The Age of Expansion
1750–1914

John D Clare

Contents

Chapter 1	The Good Old Days?	2
Chapter 2	Trade and Empire	12
Chapter 3	Population and Health	34
Chapter 4	Changes in the Economy	42
Chapter 5	Changing Attitudes	72

Nelson

The Good Old Days?

A Labourer's Life

In 1797, Sir F.M. Eden published *The State of the Poor*, a study of the standard of living of ordinary people in Britain. One family described by Eden consisted of a farm worker, his wife and four children (two of whom, aged 12 and 14, worked on local farms).

The family was quite well off – the family income was £46 a year. The table below shows the family budget. Eden was not good at maths – the total adds up to far more than £46 – but it gives us an idea of how a fairly prosperous farm worker's family lived in the eighteenth century:

Every week they bought:	£	Their yearly expenses on other things were:	£
8 large loaves (about twice as big as today's)	0.70	Soap and candles	2.36
		Fuel (mostly collected free)	1.00
2 lb* cheese	0.06	Rent	2.25
2 lb* butter	0.07	Shoes	1.50
2 lb* sugar	0.07	Clothes	4.60
2 oz** tea	0.02		
0.5 lb* oatmeal	0.15		
0.5 lb* bacon	0.15		
Milk	0.01		

* 1 lb (one pound) is about half a kilo;
** 1 oz (one ounce) is about 30 g.

QUESTIONS

1. Compare the 1797 farm labourer's weekly groceries with those bought by your own family. What do you think about his standard of living?
2. This labourer was quite well off. If his income had been the average farm worker's income of about £30 a year, how might he have saved money? Try to save 50p a week on his groceries, and £6 a year on other things. Remember, they still have to eat *something*!

A Rake's Progress

A 'rake' is a person of bad character. These pictures by the painter William Hogarth (1697–1764) tell the story of an imaginary person in the eighteenth century, but they also give us an idea of what life was like at this time.

1 The young man inherits his father's wealth.

2 In a tavern.

Chapter 1

3 Arrested for debt.

4 He marries an old maid.

5 In a gambling house.

6 In prison.

5

Chapter 1

Government

In the eighteenth century, Britain was not a democracy. Out of a population of less than 10 million people, only about 250,000 men were allowed to vote. Women were not allowed to vote. Huge towns such as Manchester and Birmingham had no MPs. Yet some places which had MPs had very few voters – they were called 'rotten boroughs'.

Parliament did not represent the people – it represented the rich.

Bribery of MPs was common. Have you heard the phrases 'before you can say Jack Robinson', and 'a golden handshake'? Mr Robinson was King George III's agent. He could (quickly and easily) get MPs to vote any way the king wanted. One way he did this was by the 'golden handshake'. As the MPs went out to cast their votes, Robinson would be waiting for them at the door. As they passed, he would shake their hands – but in his palm there would be some gold coins.

Elections were held in public, so everybody could see who you were voting for. Candidates bribed and bullied the electors.

This painting by Hogarth is called *The Election Dinner*. Study the picture. In what different ways are the candidates trying to influence the voters?

Peterloo!

In 1789, the French people revolted against their government. Before long, the new revolutionary government had sent to the guillotine the king, the queen, and any nobles and clergy they could catch.

The French Revolution scared the British government. During the eighteenth century, skilled workmen had started to combine (join together) to try to improve their working conditions; these were the first trade unions. In 1799 the government passed laws – called the Combination Acts – to stop people combining to campaign for better wages. The Combination Acts, in effect, banned trade unions.

Even after 1815, when the French were defeated at the battle of Waterloo, the government was terrified that there was going to be a revolution. In December 1816 there were riots in London. In January 1817 a man threw a stone at the Prince Regent's carriage. Parliament thought these events were the start of a revolution. In March 1817, it suspended *Habeas Corpus* (the law which stops people being imprisoned without a trial).

This did not stop the unrest. In March 1817, the poor people of Manchester planned a hunger march to London. They were called the Blanketeers, because each man carried a blanket to sleep in. There were only a few hundred marchers, and they turned back when they were told to – but the people of London thought that the entire population of Lancashire was coming down to London to murder them.

Oliver the Spy

On 9 June 1817, there was a rebellion. The rebels met at Pentrich, in Derbyshire, and marched off to attack Nottingham.

The Pentrich rebels believed that they were part of a massive rebellion. But, although they marched all night, they did not meet any other rebels. All they met, in the morning, was a small party of soldiers. Only then did they realise that they were alone. At this point they ran away, but they were easily captured; 23 of them were found guilty of treason. Most of the 23 were transported to Australia, but four were hanged.

The *Leeds Mercury* newspaper revealed soon afterwards that the rebellion had been organised by a man called William Oliver – Oliver the Spy.

Oliver was a failed builder. He had been going round the north of England, posing as a rebel leader from London. In every town he had told the workers that everyone else was ready for a revolution; they were just waiting for *that* town to rebel. The Pentrich men were the only people who had believed him.

The scandalous part of these events was that William Oliver had been in the pay of the British government. He was a spy, paid by the government to cause trouble, and then to betray the people he had encouraged to rebel.

The government had tricked people into rebelling, so that it could arrest and execute them as an example to others.

The Peterloo Massacre

Unrest continued during 1818 and 1819. The leaders were called 'Radicals', because they wanted a radical (root) change in how Britain was governed. They thought there should be a general election every year, and they wanted all men to be allowed to vote.

The Good Old Days?

A cartoon of the Peterloo Massacre. Did the cartoonist support the government or the protesters?

On 16 August 1819, a crowd of 50,000 people gathered at St Peter's Fields in Manchester to hear a speech by Mr Henry Hunt, the Radical leader. They carried banners saying 'Unity and Strength'. Everybody was wearing their Sunday best. Many men had brought their wives and families with them. One group of men arrived marching, in perfect step; they had been practising for weeks on the moors, to show the world how orderly and well-behaved working men could be. Henry Hunt's first words were to beg the crowd to stay silent and not to cause any trouble.

The authorities waited until Henry Hunt had started speaking. Then they sent in the cavalry. Some of the soldiers were drunk and lost control of their horses. Then, as the crowd tried to get away, they lashed out with their swords. Eleven people were killed and over 400 injured. The event became known as the Peterloo Massacre, a sarcastic reference to the battle of Waterloo which had taken place only four years earlier.

The Six Acts

Far from shaming the government, Peterloo convinced it that revolution was just around the corner. In 1819 it passed six acts of parliament designed to stop all chance of rebellion. The Six Acts said:

- No group of people could practise marching.
- Meetings of more than 50 people needed the permission of the local magistrates. Only local people could attend, and flags and banners were forbidden.
- Trials of troublemakers should take place quickly.
- Any house could be searched if it was suspected that it contained weapons.
- There would be strict punishments for the writers of anything criticising the government.
- Stamp duty had to be paid on all newspapers (this made them too expensive for ordinary people).

In 1820, Britain was not a free country.

Chapter 1

Changes in Britain, 1750-1914

Small island → World empire

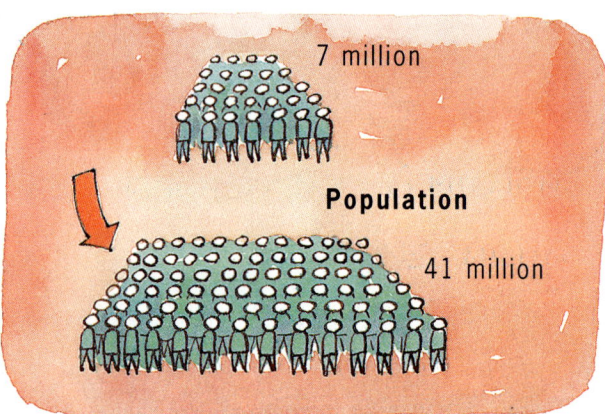

Population: 7 million → 41 million

Villages → Cities

Farming → Industry

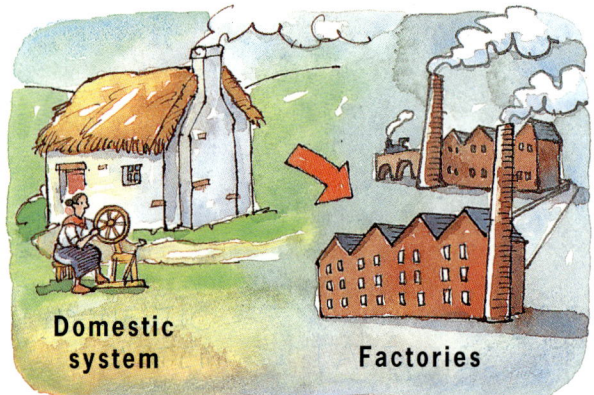

Domestic system → Factories

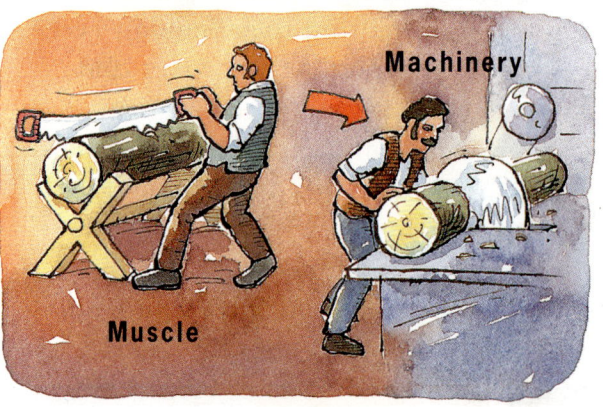

Muscle → Machinery

Transport: 5 mph → 60 mph

Poverty → Reform

An Age of Change

In the years between 1750 and 1914, Britain changed. These were the years of revolution ('turning round'), when people's lives were altered in many ways.

Britain, a small island kingdom in 1750, had become by 1914 the greatest trading nation on earth, with a worldwide empire (see Chapter 2).

During this period, there was a huge growth in population. It rose from about 7 million to 41 million. With this went a change in where people lived. Most people no longer lived in the villages and small market towns of the south of England; they lived in the great industrial towns of the north (see Chapter 3).

In 1750, Britain's economy was mainly agricultural; by 1914 the Industrial Revolution had made Britain the first industrial nation, and 'the workshop of the world' (see Chapter 4). The Industrial Revolution had many aspects. People stopped working at home on their simple hand-operated machines; by 1914 most manufactured goods were made in factories, and workers' lives were dominated by the factory chimneys and the factory clock.

Along with this went a revolution in power. In 1750, the main forms of power were clockwork and muscle power; by 1914 these had been replaced by steam power, electricity and the petrol engine. At the same time there was a revolution in transport. Horse-drawn wagons lumbering along muddy roads gave way to steam trains rushing along railway lines at 60 miles an hour.

Finally, these were the years which saw great reforms in industry and society (see Chapter 5). They were the years when slavery was abolished, when ordinary men got the vote and the right to join a trade union, and when the government passed laws to improve conditions in the factories and the cities. By the end of the nineteenth century, women also were campaigning for the vote and for equal rights with men.

Changes in everyday life

A young man, alive at this period, hardly knows what improvements of human life . . . have taken place in England since I was born – a period amounting now to nearly seventy-three years. Gas was unknown: I groped about the streets of London in all but utter darkness . . . I had no umbrella! There were no waterproof hats. I could not keep my underwear in its proper place, for braces were unknown . . . . There were no banks to take the savings of the poor; and, whatever miseries I suffered, I had no post to whisk my complaints for a single penny to the remotest corners of the empire.

Reverend Sydney Smith *(1771-1845)*

QUESTION

One historian called the years before 1750: 'The world we have lost.'

Were all the changes of the period 1750-1914 changes for the better?

Chapter 2

Trade and Empire

CLIVE IN INDIA

During the eighteenth century, Britain started to build an empire. Robert Clive was one of the men who helped to build it.

1 Robert Clive was born near Market Drayton in Shropshire in 1725. He was a lazy, naughty boy. Once he climbed the church steeple for a dare.

2 Clive and his school friends ran a protection racket amongst the town shopkeepers.

SOME SWEETS - OR YOUR WINDOWS GET BROKEN!

6 Chanda Sahib's forces defeated the British. In 1751 they besieged the important town of Trichinopoly.

7 Clive joined the East India Company army.

With 500 British and Indian soldiers, Clive captured Arcot, the capital city of the Carnatic. He hoped it would act as a diversion, so that Trichinopoly could be saved.

11 Clive went home a rich man and a hero. His father was pleased.

SO THE BOOBY OF THE FAMILY HAS SOME SENSE AFTER ALL.

12 MEANWHILE, IN INDIA: Another Indian prince, Suraj-ud-Dowlah, tried to drive out the East India Company. On 20 June 1756, he captured Calcutta in the north of India, and threw 146 Britons into prison.

13

WATER, FOR GOD'S SAKE!

THE BLACK HOLE OF CALCUTTA
Shut all night in a tiny room, without water, all but 23 of the 146 Britons died.

| 3 | In despair, his father sent him to India in 1743, to work for the East India Company. | 4 | Clive was always in trouble. He was bored and depressed. In the end he tried to shoot himself – but twice the gun failed to fire! | 5 | MEANWHILE, IN INDIA: The East India Company was in trouble. An Indian called Chanda Sahib, the Prince of the Carnatic, was trying to drive the company out of southern India. He was helped by French soldiers. |

I SEE NOW THAT I AM MEANT TO MAKE SOMETHING OF MY LIFE.

| 8 | Clive's plan worked! Chanda Sahib sent an army of 10,000 Indian soldiers to retake Arcot. | 9 | THE SIEGE OF ARCOT, 1751 The siege lasted 53 days. Food ran out. Only a little rice was left. Clive's Indian soldiers lived on the water in which the rice had been boiled. | 10 | Clive saved Trichinopoly AND held Arcot. Chanda Sahib and the French were driven out of southern India. Many Indian princes decided to support the British. |

ENGLISHMEN NEED MORE FOOD THAN WE WHO ARE USED TO HUNGER.

THE ENGLISH ARE BRAVE. I SHALL FIGHT ON THEIR SIDE.

| 14 | THE BATTLE OF PLASSEY, 1757 Clive was asked to avenge the Black Hole of Calcutta. He had an army of 3,000 men. Suraj had 15,000 horsemen, 35,000 foot-soldiers and 40 cannons. |

There was a monsoon. The British covered their gunpowder to keep it dry. Suraj's gunpowder got wet. When Suraj's cavalry attacked, they were destroyed.

| 15 |

Suraj's men fled in confusion. Only 23 of Clive's men were killed. The British now controlled Bengal, an area larger than Great Britain.

13

Chapter 2

The British Empire

Britain and France

The foundations of the British Empire were laid in the seventeenth century, when the British set up 13 colonies in North America, and some trading posts in India. They easily defeated untrained native forces armed with little more than shields and spears. Although often outnumbered, the British troops had modern weapons, and were well-trained and disciplined.

The British government soon realised the importance of its overseas empire. In 1651 it passed the Navigation Acts, which said that all trade to and from Britain had to be carried in British ships. British colonies were not allowed to make manufactured goods; instead, they had to buy them from Britain. This meant that British merchants could make vast fortunes selling machinery, clothes and hardware to the colonists; then they could make just as much money bringing back furs, sugar, tobacco and tea from the colonies!

Britain's main rival was France. France was much bigger and wealthier than Britain. Its army was more powerful than the small British army.

But Britain had a number of advantages over France. British traders could go on trading voyages whenever they wanted. When they became wealthy, they were often elected to be Members of Parliament. This meant that they had a say in the government's decisions. In France, all trading ventures were controlled by the king. Even the richest merchants were despised by the nobles.

It was even more important that Britain was an island. France was often involved in wars in Europe. The British learned to ignore events in Europe, and to concentrate on building up their empire overseas.

Below: Captain Cook explored Australia and New Zealand in 1768-79. After 1788, Britain transported many convicts to Australia, which was used as a huge prison.

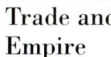

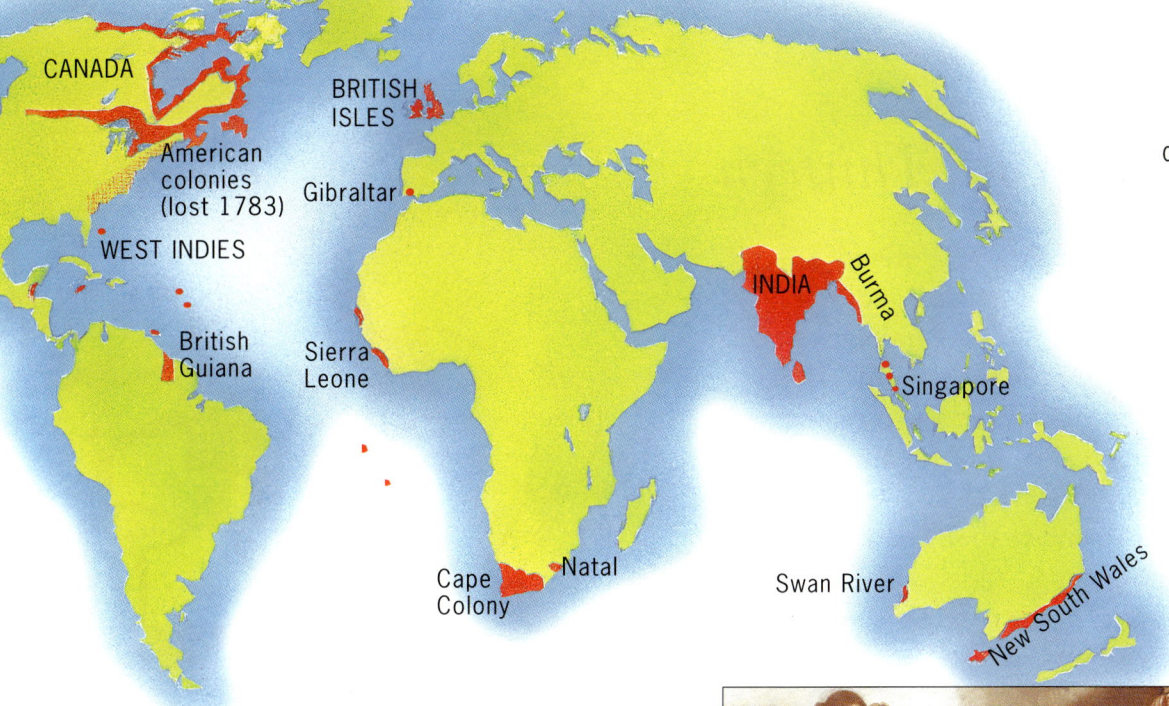

Above: The British Empire in 1830.

Below: The death of Wolfe at Quebec. It was reported that when he was told that the French were fleeing, Wolfe's last words were, 'Now I die content.'

The Seven Years' War (1756-63)

The Seven Years' War was a conflict between Britain and France, but British troops did little fighting in Europe. Instead, the British sent money to their ally, Frederick of Prussia, to help him fight the French. The British fought mainly to increase their empire.

Britain's greatest triumphs came in 1759, the 'Wonderful Year'. The British navy was more powerful than the French navy. In 1759, it destroyed the French fleet. For the rest of the war, therefore, British troops around the world could be supplied and reinforced by the British navy, whereas the French troops had no such support.

As a result, Britain's empire grew during the war. In India, Robert Clive won the Battle of Plassey (see page 13).

The British were also able to destroy French power in America. In 1759, a British army under General James Wolfe attacked the French headquarters at Quebec in Canada. At first it seemed as though he was going to fail. Then one night Wolfe led his men up the steep cliffs which protected Quebec. In the battle that followed, both Wolfe and the French commander were killed. French influence in North America was ended.

At the Treaty of Paris, which ended the war in 1763, the French gave up Canada and most of their power in India. The British also captured a number of islands in the West Indies — at this time, the tobacco and sugar they produced made them the most profitable places on earth. Britain also took land in Africa and the Far East.

The money which came from trade and the Empire made Britain the wealthiest nation on earth, and was a cause of the Industrial Revolution (see Chapter 4).

Chapter 2

Unlucky Thirteen

In 1783, the British Empire suffered a setback when the 13 American colonies fought and won the War of Independence. The conflict arose because the British government thought that the American colonists ought to help pay for the wars against France, which had been very costly. It tried to make them pay customs duties on paint, paper, glass and tea. The colonists did not want to pay.

On 16 December 1773, therefore, a group of American colonists dressed up as American Indians. They boarded British ships in Boston harbour and threw their cargo of tea into the sea (the 'Boston Tea Party'). On 5 September 1774, the American leaders met in Philadelphia and decided to resist the British government.

In the war that followed, the Americans, led by George Washington and helped by the French, defeated the British. In 1783, Britain was forced to accept the independence of the United States.

Above: George Washington.

1 An American poem of 1773

There was an old lady lived
  over the sea,
And she was an Island Queen;
Her daughter lived off in a new country,
With an ocean of water between.
The old lady's pockets were full of gold,
And never contented was she,
So she called on her daughter to pay
  her a tax
Of three pence a pound on her tea.

2 The Declaration of Independence

We hold these truths to be self-evident, that all men are created equal, that they are endowed by their Creator with certain unalienable rights, that among these are Life, Liberty and the Pursuit of Happiness . . . . That whenever any Government becomes destructive of these ends, it is the Right of the People to alter or abolish it . . . .

Thomas Jefferson, *4 July 1776*

? ? ? QUESTIONS ? ?

1. What does source 1 suggest was the cause of the American Revolution?
2. What does the Declaration of Independence imply was the cause?
3. Explain why the two are so different.

The American War of Independence

There were 13 main incidents in the war:

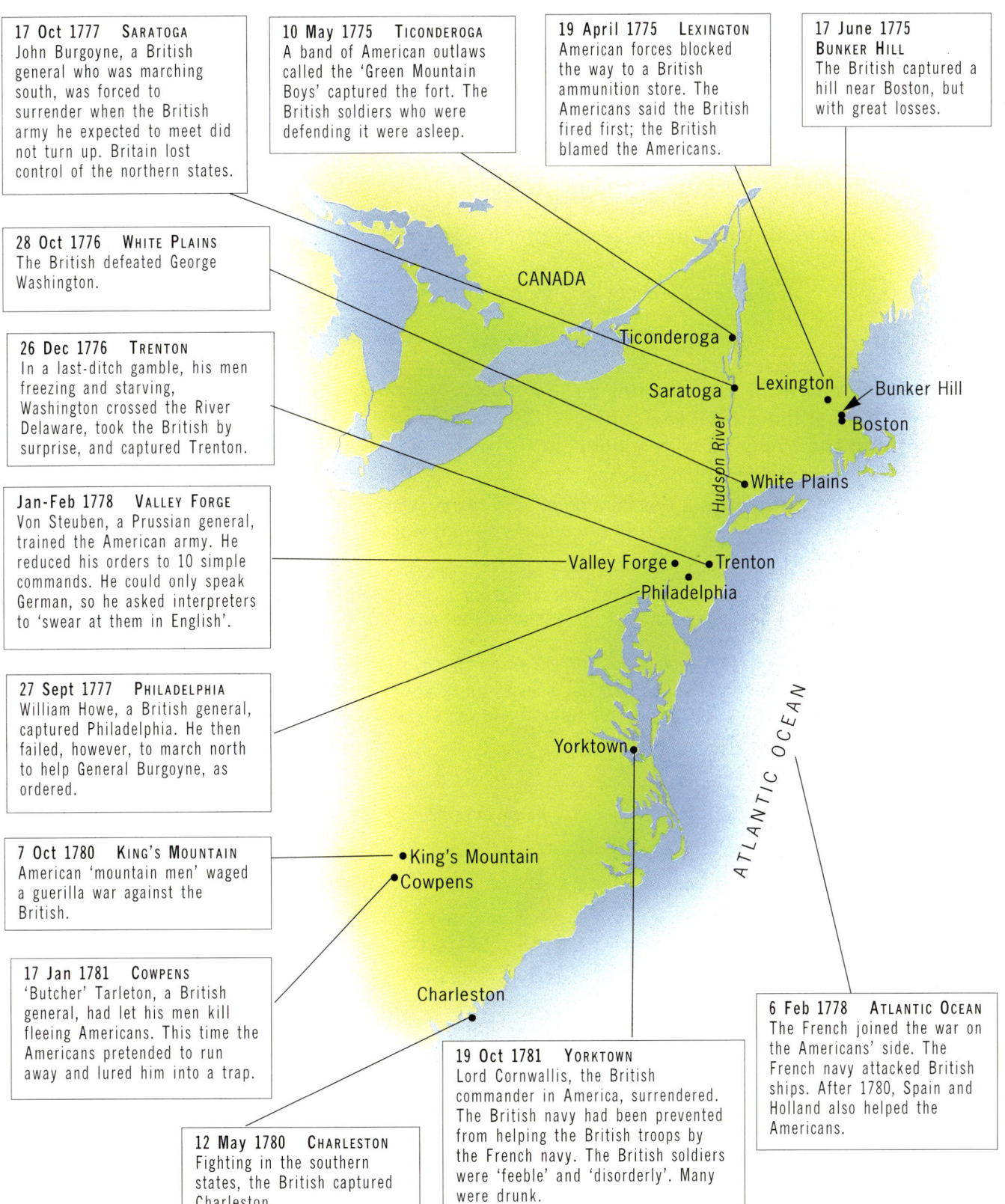

17 Oct 1777 SARATOGA
John Burgoyne, a British general who was marching south, was forced to surrender when the British army he expected to meet did not turn up. Britain lost control of the northern states.

28 Oct 1776 WHITE PLAINS
The British defeated George Washington.

26 Dec 1776 TRENTON
In a last-ditch gamble, his men freezing and starving, Washington crossed the River Delaware, took the British by surprise, and captured Trenton.

Jan-Feb 1778 VALLEY FORGE
Von Steuben, a Prussian general, trained the American army. He reduced his orders to 10 simple commands. He could only speak German, so he asked interpreters to 'swear at them in English'.

27 Sept 1777 PHILADELPHIA
William Howe, a British general, captured Philadelphia. He then failed, however, to march north to help General Burgoyne, as ordered.

7 Oct 1780 KING'S MOUNTAIN
American 'mountain men' waged a guerilla war against the British.

17 Jan 1781 COWPENS
'Butcher' Tarleton, a British general, had let his men kill fleeing Americans. This time the Americans pretended to run away and lured him into a trap.

10 May 1775 TICONDEROGA
A band of American outlaws called the 'Green Mountain Boys' captured the fort. The British soldiers who were defending it were asleep.

19 April 1775 LEXINGTON
American forces blocked the way to a British ammunition store. The Americans said the British fired first; the British blamed the Americans.

17 June 1775 BUNKER HILL
The British captured a hill near Boston, but with great losses.

12 May 1780 CHARLESTON
Fighting in the southern states, the British captured Charleston.

19 Oct 1781 YORKTOWN
Lord Cornwallis, the British commander in America, surrendered. The British navy had been prevented from helping the British troops by the French navy. The British soldiers were 'feeble' and 'disorderly'. Many were drunk.

6 Feb 1778 ATLANTIC OCEAN
The French joined the war on the Americans' side. The French navy attacked British ships. After 1780, Spain and Holland also helped the Americans.

Trade and Empire

17

Chapter 2

Why Did Britain Lose?

Historians have suggested many reasons why Britain lost the American War of Independence. The sources on these two pages will help you form your own opinion.

> **1** Never had the British army so ungenerous an enemy. They send their riflemen 5 or 6 at a time, who hide themselves behind trees, till an opportunity presents itself of taking a shot at our men. Then they immediately retreat. What an unfair way of carrying on a war.
>
> *A British officer who fought in the war.*

> **2** No European army would suffer a fraction of what the Americans suffer. It takes citizens to put up with hunger, nakedness, toil, and total lack of pay.
>
> **Lafayette**, *a French soldier who helped the Americans during the war.*

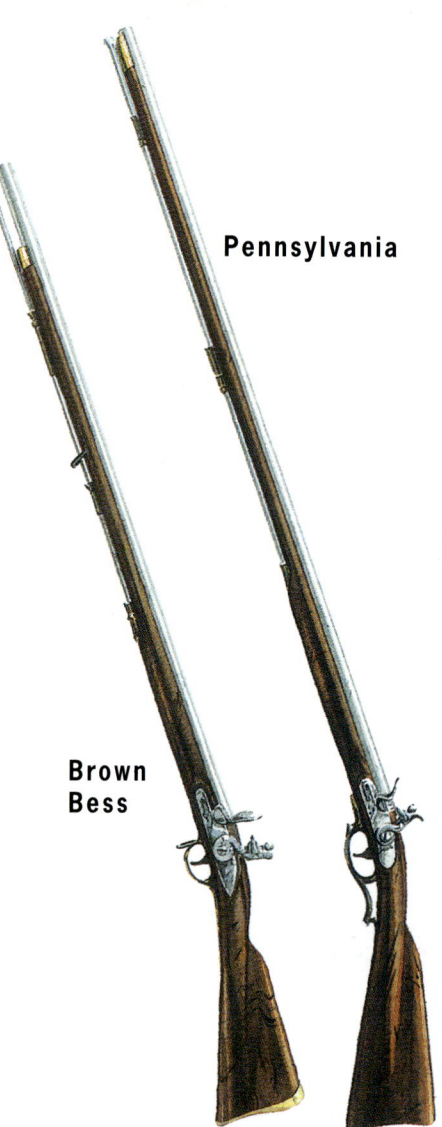

3 The firing range of the guns used in the war. Position 1 shows the distance at which a soldier could expect to hit what he was aiming at. Position 2 shows the maximum distance at which the gun might wound an enemy soldier.

Many Americans used the Pennsylvania rifle, made by German gunsmiths in North America. Most British soldiers used the 'Brown Bess', which had been invented in about 1700. A Scottish soldier, Patrick Ferguson, had developed a better rifle, but General Howe refused permission for it to be used, because Ferguson had not asked him first.

Type	Calibre (Inches)	Range in yards 50	100	150	200	250
 Brown Bess	.753		1		2	
 Pennsylvania	.40-60				1	2

18

Trade and Empire

4 In this cartoon of the time, the cow stands for the British Empire, the lion for the British people, the warship for the British navy and the dog for troublemakers in Britain.

The cartoon shows the Americans cutting the horns from the cow, while France, Spain and Holland happily steal her milk. The British lion sleeps, ignoring both the dog and the man begging it to wake up. In the background, the British warship – without guns or rudder – has run aground.

5 We meant well to the Americans – just to punish them with a few bloody noses, and then to make laws for the happiness of both countries. But lack of discipline got into the army, lack of skill and energy in the navy, and lack of unity at home. We lost America.

George III, *King of England, 1760-1820.*

QUESTIONS

1 Look at sources 1-5. Give each source a suitable title.
2 Look at the main events of the war on page 17. Read about the events, and suggest other reasons why the British lost the war.

Chapter 2

The Slave Trade

There were slaves in the time of the Ancient Egyptians and the Ancient Greeks. The Romans owned slaves. But it is shameful to think that, until 1807, British traders also bought and sold human beings.

The slave trade took place on a vast scale. Between 1450 and 1850, about 14 million Africans were taken from their homes to become slaves in the New World. At least the same number were killed in the wars that accompanied the slave trade, or died during the journey across the Atlantic.

The slave trade damaged life in Africa. Slaving parties roamed the country taking the youngest and healthiest members of the community. Faced with the daily danger of death or capture, some Africans stopped bothering to grow food or make clothes. Some parents sold their children for a few bottles of brandy.

At the same time, in America and the West Indies, slavery de-humanised both owners and slaves. The owners were racist in a way that takes our breath away today.

At the end of the eighteenth century, however, attitudes in Britain and the United States began to change. People began to realise that it is wrong for one person to own another.

The Campaign for Abolition

The leader of the campaign to abolish slavery was William Wilberforce. Each year, from 1788 to 1807, Wilberforce presented a Bill to the British Parliament calling for the abolition of the slave trade. For 18 years, his Bill was defeated.

The abolitionists decided to get public opinion on their side. They produced leaflets and books; they travelled round the country giving speeches. The campaign against slavery was the first ever public campaign for reform.

In the end, the abolitionists won. They changed people's opinions. The slave trade in the British Empire was abolished in 1807, and slavery was abolished in 1833. The British then spent the nineteenth century trying to persuade the rest of the world to abolish slavery.

The abolitionists' campaign slogan was the slaves' claim that all men and women are equal.

Unloading sugar and rum at the West India Docks in London.

The Triangular Trade

The slave trade involved a voyage of three stages. For this reason, it is sometimes called 'the triangular trade'.

The British wanted the produce of the West Indies: sugar, rum, cotton and tobacco. The planters of the West Indies were short of workers. As for the Africans, one of their tribal chiefs summed up their situation:

We lack three things: powder, shot [lead bullets] and brandy. We have three things to sell: men, women and children.

Slaving ships sailed from one of the ports connected with the slave trade, mainly London, Bristol and Liverpool. Their cargoes included cloth, hats and caps, iron bars, all sorts of hardware from swords to saucepans, guns, shot and gunpowder, salt, and worthless trinkets such as beads and bells.

This cargo was taken to ports such as Benin in Africa, where it was exchanged for slaves. The ships then sailed to America, or Barbados and Jamaica in the West Indies, where the slaves were sold (the voyage across the Atlantic was called 'the Middle Passage'). The slave traders were sometimes paid in cash, but often they took payment in kind, returning with sugar, rum, cotton or tobacco to sell in Britain.

The slave trade was very profitable, but there were risks at every stage. In Africa there might not be a cargo of slaves ready, and the crew could fall ill or be attacked while they waited. On the Middle Passage there was a chance of epidemic or mutiny; it was usual for a third of the slaves to die. Finally, the slave trader might arrive back in Britain to find that he could not sell his cargo at a profit because there was a glut on the market.

Chapter 2

Africa

What was Africa like when the slave traders first went there? The sources on these two pages will allow you to come to your own conclusion.

> **1** I was born, in 1745, in the kingdom of Benin, in a charming, fruitful valley.
>
> Our manner of living is entirely plain . . . bullocks, goats and poultry supply most of our food . . . . Before we taste the food we always wash our hands; indeed, our cleanliness at all times is extreme . . . . We have no strong or alcoholic liquors; our main drink is palm wine . . . .
>
> Our wants are few and easily supplied; of course we have few manufactures. They consist for the most part of cloth, pottery, ornaments and instruments of war and farming . . . .
>
> Our land is uncommonly rich and fruitful, and produces all kinds of vegetables in great abundance . . . . Agriculture is our chief employment; and everyone, even the children and women, are engaged in it. Thus we are all used to work from our earliest years. Everyone contributes to the common welfare; and, as we do not know idleness, we have no beggars . . . .
>
> The West Indian planters prefer the slaves of Benin to those of any other part of Africa, for their hardiness, intelligence, honesty and zeal.
>
> **Olaudah Equiano**, *The Interesting Narrative of the Life of Olaudah Equiano* (1789)

2 The procession of the Oba (king) of Benin in 1668. In the front are musicians, followed by the warriors and the townspeople. The town of Benin is in the background.

3 They were a people of beastly living, without God, law, religion, or community.

John Lok, *a slave factor (seller of slaves), 1554.*

4 Extremely lazy ... full of treachery and lies ... and addicted to stealing.

William Snelgrave, *the captain of a slave-trading ship (1734).*

5 The Negroes are all, without exception, crafty, villainous, fraudulent, and very seldom to be trusted, being sure to miss no opportunity of cheating a European, nor indeed, one another.... They are besides incredibly careless and stupid.

H. Bosman, *a Dutch slave trader who spent 14 years in Africa (1839).*

6 Every eighth day is Calabar Sunday, when they drink mimbo [palm wine] all day long; and at night there is not a sober man or woman in the town unless they cannot get mimbo. The next day they sleep all day long.

Captain Nicholas, *speaking to the Africa Association (18th century).*

7 Many Europeans described the cruelty of the African rulers. This is a drawing of a human sacrifice ordered by the King of Dahomey, in West Africa. It appeared in 1879 in the French *Journal of Travel – Adventures on Sea and Land*, a magazine full of exciting stories written by travellers.

8 I was surprised to see the land so well cultivated; the lowlands divided by small canals, all sowed with rice; their beef excellent, poultry numerous.... [They are] kind to strangers with whom they are fond of trading... [although] the frequent wrongs done them by Europeans have led to them being suspicious and shy.

Bue, *a French traveller (18th century).*

9 [The people of Benin] are a gentle, loving people ... who do not hurt anyone, especially strangers....

Samuel Purchas, *an English traveller (18th century).*

??? QUESTION ???

Suggest reasons why the description of Africa and the Africans in source 1 is so different from those in sources 3-7.

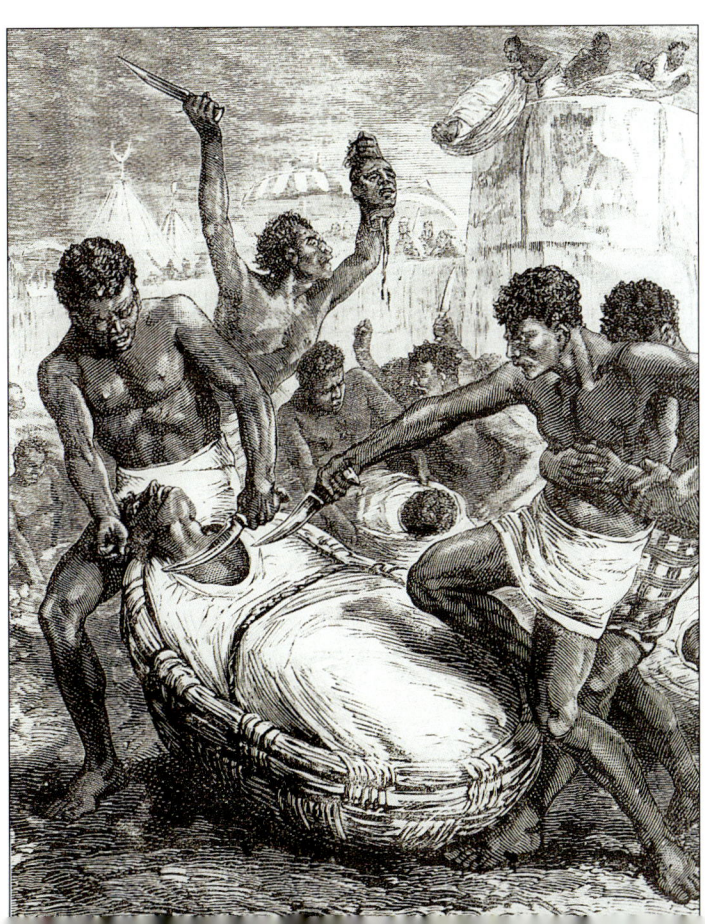

Chapter 2

Captured!

In the early days of the slave trade, white slave traders (called 'blackbirders') simply landed anywhere on the African coast, chased after Africans and caught them. This was called Lesser Pillage. Later, the British traders used middlemen called slave factors. The factors made agreements with local African rulers, who declared war on their neighbours, took prisoners of war, and then sold their captives as slaves to the factors. This was called Grand Pillage.

> **1** I had become friends with some other children, and we were some days too bold in going into the woods to gather fruit and catch birds . . . . One day we went into the woods as usual, but we had not been above two hours, before our troubles began, when several ruffians came upon us suddenly.
>
> Some of us tried in vain to run away, but pistols and cutlasses were soon produced, threatening that if we tried to move we should all lie dead on the spot. One of them pretended to be more friendly than the rest, and said he would speak to their lord to get us clear, and desired that we should follow him; we were then immediately divided into different parties, and were driven after him. We were soon led out of the way which we knew, into slavery.
>
> **Ottobah Cuguano**, *Thoughts on the Evil and Wicked Traffic of Slavery (1787)*

> **2** On attacking a place it is the custom of the country instantly to set fire to it; and as they are all made of straw huts only, the whole is soon devoured by the flames. The unfortunate inhabitants run quickly from the fire and fall immediately into the hands of their no less merciless enemies who surround the place; the men are quickly massacred, and the women and children lashed together and made slaves.
>
> **Major Denham** *(18th century)*

3 Captured slaves were taken to the coast in lines called *coffles* (from the Arab word *cafila*, meaning 'a caravan'). They would be whipped and made to run about 20 miles a day.

Trade and Empire

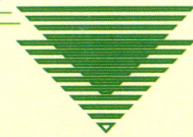

4 A slave raid. The slave traders in this picture are Arabs. They are dressed in white robes. Which Africans are the slave traders NOT taking? Suggest reasons for their choice.

5 One young woman had (for the first time) become a mother two days only before she was taken, and her child, being thought by her captor too young to be worth saving, was thrown by the monster into the burning hut, from which the flames had just obliged the mother to retreat.
William Gray
(18th century)

6 Slave traders sometimes took pawns (hostages) in order to get a better deal.

I hope you and merchant Black won't stay away, or the other merchants of Liverpool that has a mind to send their ships. They shall be used with nothing but civility and fair trade. Other Captains may say what they please about my doing them any bad thing, for what I did was their own faults, for you may think, sir, that it was very annoying to have my sons carried off by Capt. Jackson . . . . And to annoy us more the time we were firing at each other they hanged one of our sons from the yard-arm . . . .
Your best friend, **Grandy King George**.
Letter from a Calabari caboceer (local ruler) to a Liverpool trading company.

25

Chapter 2

The Price of a Slave

Haggling over the price of a slave.

By 1800, British slave ships sailed to the African coast and tried to buy a cargo of slaves from a factor, or direct from an African ruler. The passage on the right describes what one slave-trading captain said that he paid for slaves in 1801.

Captain Crow's estimate of the price of a slave at Bonny Bay in 1801:

About 100 metres of different types of cloth, forty-five handkerchiefs;
One large brass pan, two muskets;
Twenty-five kegs of powder, one hundred flints;
Two bags of shot, twenty knives;
Four iron pots, four hats, four caps;
Four cutlasses, six hundred bunches of beads, fourteen gallons of brandy.
These articles cost about £25, so that the reader will see we do not get Negroes (as many have supposed) for nothing.

Quoted in **P. Richardson**, *Empire and Slavery (1968)*

As the selling price of a good slave was only about £35 in America, it is possible that Captain Crow was exaggerating. Captain Crow was a good slave trader, who treated his cargo well. When he docked in the West Indies, many of his former 'passengers' went to the docks to say hello!

Trade and Empire

The Middle Passage

What were conditions like on the voyage from Africa to America and the West Indies?

1 We recommend you to treat the Negroes with as much care as safety will allow and let none of your men abuse them under any pretence whatsoever. Be sure you see their victuals [food] well made and given them in due season.... We recommend you to make fires frequently in the Negroes' rooms.... We recommend mutton broth....

Instructions from the owners of the ship Africa *to Captain George Merrick, 1774.*

2 [The slaves were laid] in two rows one above the other, on each side of the ship, close to each other, like books upon a shelf. I have known them so close that the shelf would not easily contain one more. And I have known a white man sent down among the men to lay them in rows to the greatest advantage, so that as little space as possible be lost....

And every morning perhaps more instances than one are found of the living and the dead ... fastened together.

John Newton, *Thoughts Upon the African Slave Trade* (1788)

3 I am growing sicker every day of this business of buying and selling human beings for beasts of burden.... On the eighth day [out at sea] I took my round of the half deck, holding a camphor bag in my teeth; for the stench was hideous. The sick and dying were chained together. I saw pregnant women give birth to babies whilst chained to corpses, which our drunken overseers had not removed. The blacks were literally jammed between decks as if in a coffin, and a coffin that dreadful hold became to nearly one half of our cargo before we reached Bahia [in Brazil].

Richard Drake, *Revelations of a Slave Smuggler* (1860)

4 An illustration showing how slaves were made to lie in a slave ship. The slaves on this ship had less than 76 centimetres of headroom.

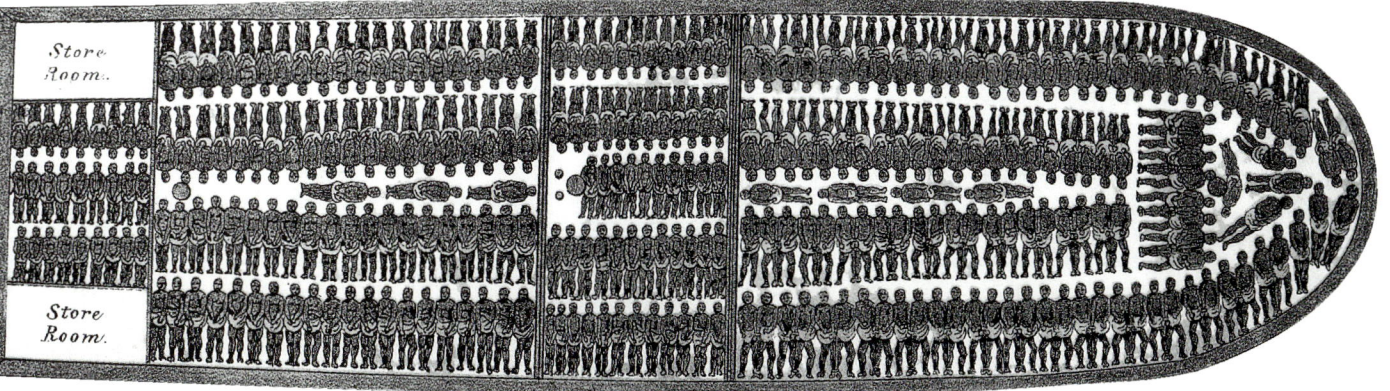

27

Chapter 2

5 A painting of the hold of the slave ship *Albanes*, after its capture (19th century).

6 We spent in our passage from St Thomas to Barbados two months eleven days . . . in which time there happened much sickness and death among my poor men and Negroes, that of the first we buried 14, and of the last, 320 . . . whereby the loss in all amounted to £6,560.

    Captain Thomas Phillips, *A Voyage Made in the Hannibal, 1693-94* (1732). Captain Phillips was a slave trader.

7 Some wet and blowing weather having caused the port-holes to be shut, fluxes [dysentery] and fevers among the Negroes followed. I often went down among them, till at length their apartments became so excessively hot as to be only bearable for a very short time . . . .

  The floor of their rooms was so covered in the blood and mucus which had come from them because of the flux that it was like a slaughter-house . . . .

    Alexander Falconbridge, *An Account of the Slave Trade* (1788). Falconbridge was a ship's doctor.

8 There was nothing to be heard but the rattling of chains, smacking of whips, and the groans and cries of our fellow-men . . . . Death was preferable to life, and a plan was made to blow up the ship . . . but we were betrayed.

    Ottobah Cuguano, *Thoughts on the Evil and Wicked Traffic of Slavery* (1787)

9 The slaves in the night were often heard making a howling melancholy kind of noise, something expressive of extreme anguish.

    Dr Trotter (1784)

Trade and Empire

10 Slaves were taken in small numbers up on deck, and whipped to make them exercise.

11 To our great amazement above 100 men slaves jumped overboard . . . we lost 3 good men slaves, who would not try to save themselves, but resolved to die and sunk directly down . . . .

Captain Japhet Bird, *Boston Weekly News Letter (April 1737)*

12 We had half the gang on deck today for exercise; they danced and sang, under the driver's whip, but are far from sprightly . . . .
  Last Tuesday the smallpox began to rage, and we hauled 60 corpses out of the hold . . . . We bribed the blacks with rum in order to get their help in removing corpses. The sights which I witnessed may I never look on such again. This is a dreadful trade. Some of the blacks are raving mad, and screech like wild beasts.

Richard Drake, *Revelations of a Slave Smuggler (1860)*

13 Slavery continued in the United States until 1863. In 1839 slaves on the ship *Amistad* killed the captain and the cook and ordered the crew to sail back to Africa. Instead, the crew sailed to New York, where the slaves were arrested. They were freed, however, when they proved that they had been kidnapped.

29

Chapter 2

Slaves for Sale

When a slave ship arrived in America or the West Indies, the slaves were fattened up for sale, and their skins were oiled to make them shine. Traders hid sores by rubbing them with rust, and slaves with dysentery were 'plugged' with rope dipped in tar.

4 A slave sale in America, from *The Life and Adventures of Henry Bibb, Written by Himself* (1849). Bibb was a black American who had been a slave.

1 Such a resurrection of skin and bones, as . . . appeared to be risen from the grave . . . walking skeletons covered over with a piece of tanned leather.
  Captain Stedman (?1796), *a slave trader.*

2 They were crouched down upon their benches around a large room; during a visit of more than an hour not a word was spoken. They were nearly all naked . . . with a few exceptions they were but skin and bone, too weak to support their weary bodies . . . .
  Dr Cullen (*18th century*)

3 They seemed past all hope of recovery. God knows what we shall do with what remain, they are a most scabby flock, all of them full of sores – some have extreme sore eyes, three very puny children and add to this the worst infirmity of all with which 6 or 8 are attended (i.e.) Old Age.
  Letter from **Henry Laurens**, *a slave trader, to Vernon Brothers, Newport (1756).*

5 They show on being brought to the market very few signs of sadness for their past, or fears for their future; but a great eagerness to be sold . . . and appearing disappointed when refused.
  Bryan Edwards, *History of the British West Indies* (1819)

6 Tuesday, September 13th, 1774
Went ashore and saw a Cargo of Slaves land. One of the most shocking sights I ever saw. About 400 Men, Women, and Children, brought from their native Country, deprived of their liberty, and themselves and their children become the property of cruel strangers without a chance of ever enjoying the Blessings of Freedom again, or a right of complaining, be their sufferings never so great . . . . They were all naked, except a piece of blue cloth about a foot broad to cover their nakedness, and appear much dejected.
  Nicholas Cresswell, *Journal* (1774-7)

Trade and Empire

7 As soon as the hour agreed on arrived, the doors of the yard were suddenly thrown open, and in rushed a considerable number of purchasers, with all the ferocity of beasts.... Some instantly seized such Negroes as they could conveniently lay hold of with their hands. Others, being prepared with several handkerchiefs tied together, encircled with these as many as they were able....

The Negroes appeared extremely terrified, and near thirty of them jumped into the sea. But they were all soon retaken....

Alexander Falconbridge, *An Account of the Slave Trade (1788)*

9 *Above:* A slave sale, illustrated in Wilson Armistead's *Five Thousand Strokes for Freedom*, published by the Leeds Anti-Slavery Society in 1853.

8 *Below:* In the West Indies, the slaves were sold at a sale called a 'scramble'. Women fetched the highest prices, especially if they had children.

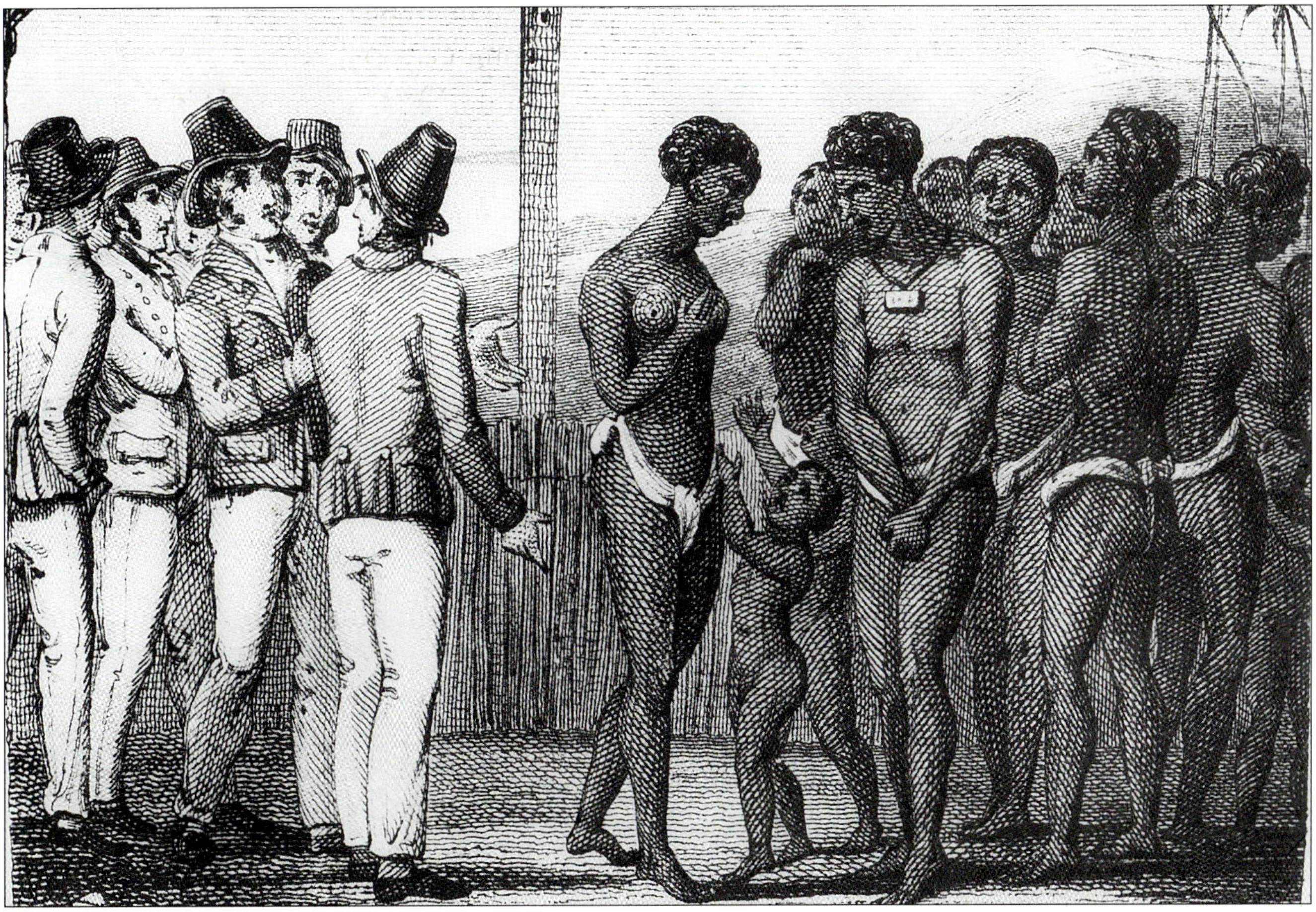

31

Attitudes to Empire

In the nineteenth century, the British Empire continued to grow. There was a 'scramble' for colonies, especially in Africa. By 1900 the British Empire had become 'the empire on which the sun never set'. It provided food for Britain's population, raw materials for Britain's factories and markets for British products. The Empire made Britain rich.

What did the British think about their empire and its peoples?

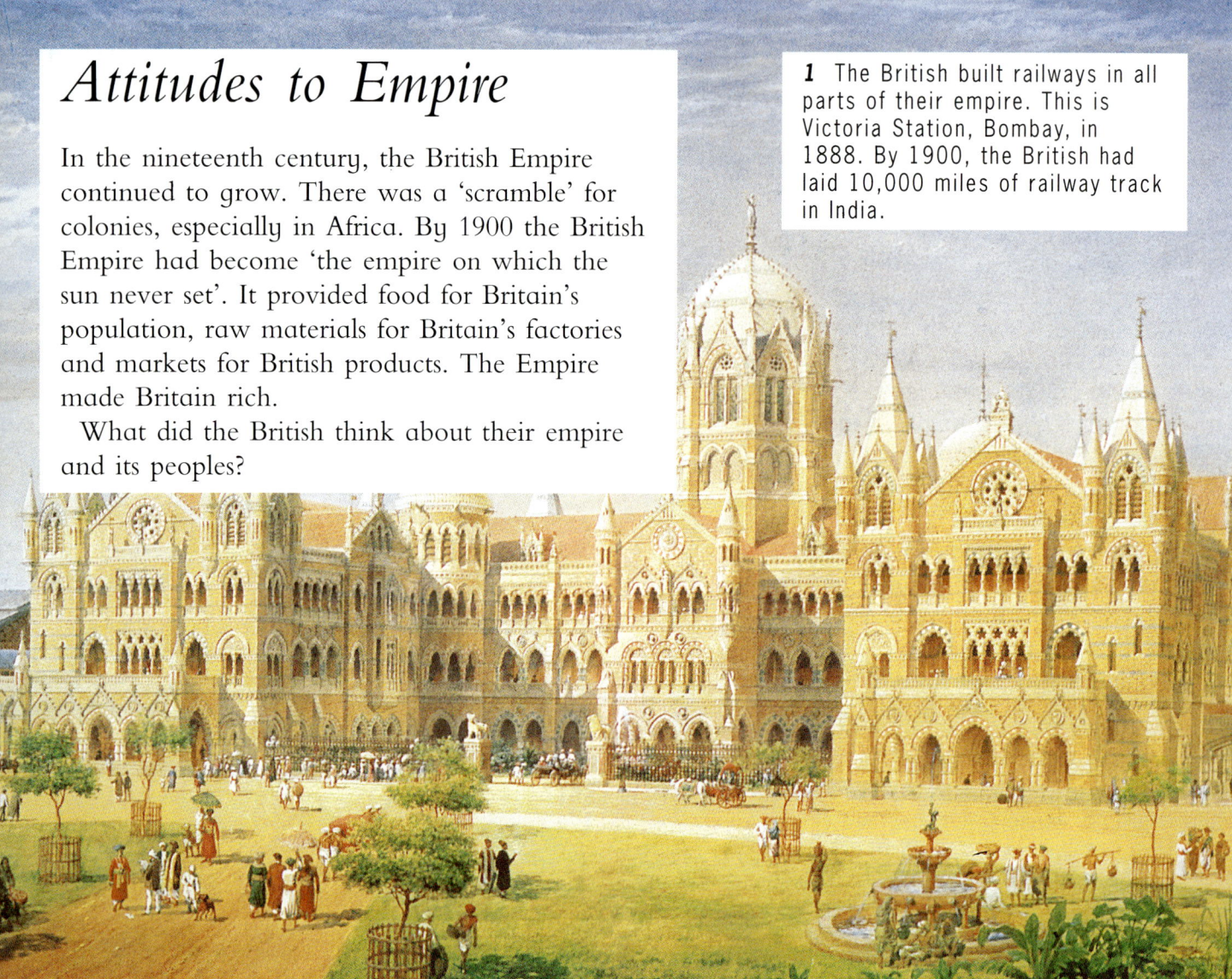

1 The British built railways in all parts of their empire. This is Victoria Station, Bombay, in 1888. By 1900, the British had laid 10,000 miles of railway track in India.

2 One of the wonderful stories of history is that which tells how a little group of islands [the British Isles] . . . became the Motherland of the greatest Empire the world has ever seen . . . .

There must be something remarkable about these islands which have become the centre of an Empire which covers about one-fifth of the lands of the globe and is the home of at least a quarter of the world's people.

Newnes' Pictorial Knowledge (1930s). A children's encyclopaedia.

3 Law and order is perhaps the most important advantage that we British gave to our colonies . . . . We took the ideas of liberty, equality, justice and democracy to the colonies. With these came the advantages of civilisation, closely followed by the benefits of technology.

What were these advantages? First – ease of travel, secondly – education, thirdly – public health. In addition to the fight against disease, our experts helped to provide sanitation and pure water supplies. Also there were improvements in agriculture.

A British Official (20th century).

4 If the native people rebelled, European soldiers killed and tortured them. The profits of the colonies did not go to benefit the native people, who were desperately poor, and whose cheap labour allowed the big profits to be made. Instead, they went to the wealthy shareholders in London.

Finally, there was the constant and needless humiliation of the natives. Almost all Europeans took it for granted that they, the Whites, were a superior people who automatically deserved the respect and service of the coloured races whom they ruled.

M. Roberts, *Machines and Liberty (1972). An A-level textbook.*

5 From Greenland's
  icy mountains,
From India's coral strand
Where Africa's sunny fountains
Roll down their golden sand . . . .
In vain with lavish kindness
The gifts of God are strown;
The heathen in his blindness
Bows down to wood and stone.

Can we, whose souls are lighted
With wisdom from on high,
Can we to men benighted
The lamp of life deny?
Salvation! O salvation!
The joyful sound proclaim,
Till each remotest nation
  has learned Messiah's name.

Bishop R. Heber *(1783-1826)*

Heathen: not Christian.
Benighted: backward, ignorant.
Messiah: Jesus Christ.

Trade and Empire

6 An educated native once complained to me that most Englishmen seemed to him to walk about the world with an air as if God intended the whole universe to be English.

Monier Williams, *Modern India (1878). Williams visited India in 1875.*

7 We are the British, engaged in the magnificent work of governing an inferior race.

Lord Mayo, *Viceroy of India 1869-72. In 1872 he was assassinated by an Indian.*

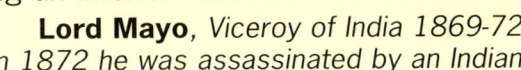
QUESTIONS

Look at the sources on these pages.
Is there anything Britain can be proud of?
Is there anything to be ashamed of?

8 A British man returning from a hunt in Mysore, India, in 1892.

Chapter 3

Population and Health

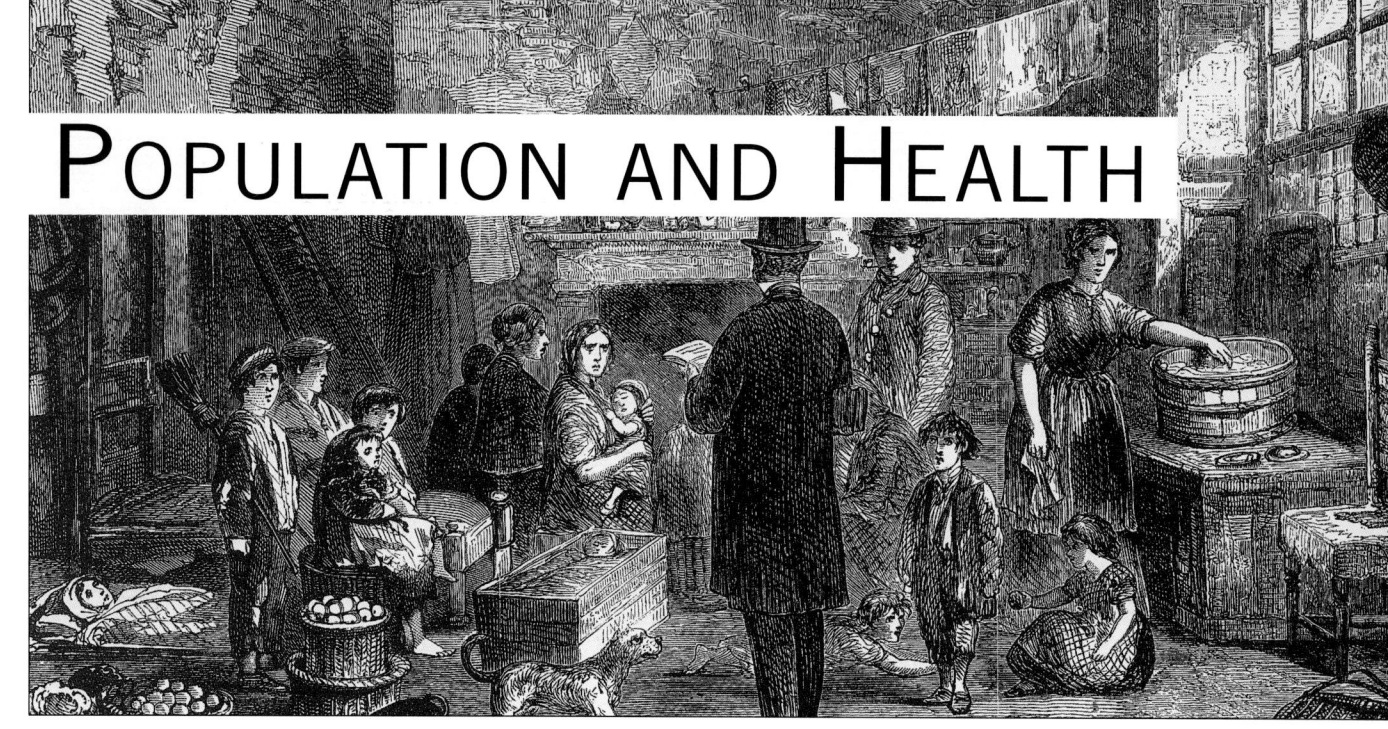

After 1801, the government started to take a census (a counting of the population) every ten years. As most people could not read or write, census enumerators visited each house and listed the people who lived there. After 1850, they also noted down details such as marital status (whether people were married or unmarried), age, occupation and place of birth.

Here, a census enumerator takes a census in a London house in 1861. The enumerators were only human. What kind of mistakes might have got into the final census?

During the eighteenth century, Britain's population started to grow. Nobody knows exactly when – there are no reliable figures available – but in the years between 1700 and 1800 the population rose from about 6 million to 11 million.

The growing population needed food, clothes, houses, fuel and a great number of other goods and services such as shops, churches and public houses. This growing demand was one of the causes of the Industrial Revolution (see Chapter 4).

Census enumerator's returns for a house in the small village of Middridge, County Durham, in 1851.

Name	Position	Status	Age	Occupation	Place of Birth
Thomas Bainbridge	Head	M	74	Farmer of 210 acres employing 2 labourers	Bowes, Yorkshire
Jane "	Wife	M	70		Middleton, Durham
Jacob "	Son	M	33	Farmer	Mickleton, Durham
Jane "	Wife	M	31		Easington, Durham
Jacob Tarn "	Son		3		Bowes, Yorkshire
Robert "	Son		1		Middridge, Durham
Sythia Dent	Gr. Dau.		13		Brough, Westmorland
Thomas Wilkinson	Servant	U	21	Farm Servant	Hamsterley, Durham
Thomas Matthews	Servant	U	20	" "	Heighington, Durham

34

Why Did the Population Grow?

In 1798 a vicar called Thomas Malthus wrote *An Essay on the Principle of Population*. He forecast war, disease and famine, if the number of people continued to grow. In fact, in the past there had always been a 'population ceiling' beyond which numbers could not grow. But by 1800 Malthus's ideas were no longer correct. The population continued growing. It reached 21 million in 1851, and 37 million by 1901.

Nobody knows why the population grew, but historians have made many suggestions. Some of these are listed below:

1 Agricultural Changes
Changes in farming in the 18th century helped farmers to produce more food - notably milk, cheese and vegetables.

2 Changes in Fashion
After 1750 people started to wear cotton, instead of woollen, underwear. Cotton was easier to wash.

3 Climate Changes
After 1780, the weather began to get warmer, which helped the farmers.

4 Medical Changes
In the 18th century there were improvements in midwifery and the care of pregnant women.

5 Vaccination
Vaccination was discovered in 1796. People who were vaccinated against smallpox were immune to the disease.

6 Behavioural Changes
After 1700 people married earlier, and fewer people stayed unmarried.

7 Personal Hygiene
After 1790, soap became easily available and was cheaper.

8 Cultural Changes
At the start of the 18th century, there was a craze for gin drinking. This died out after the government began to tax gin in 1751. Gin can cause miscarriages and can damage unborn babies.

9 Environmental Changes
At the start of the 18th century, many marshes were drained; this killed the mosquitoes, so fewer people got malaria.

10 Government Action
The Public Health Acts in 1848 and 1875 improved housing and public health in towns.

11 Factories
After 1780, more children were employed in factories. Children were useful because they earned a wage.

??? QUESTIONS ???

1. Which of the causes listed here would have helped to reduce the death rate (the number of deaths)?
2. Which would have helped to increase the birth rate (the number of births)?
3. How might they have done this?

Overleaf: Ordnance Survey maps of Eldon, in County Durham, for 1857 and 1897.

1897

90
6.233

92
5.240

93
2.445

Methodist Chapel
(Primitive)

89
2.149

94
13.398

Close House

94a
4.680

Royal Hotel
(P.H.)

Post Office

S.S.

93
1.78

94
.338

95
2.286

95
2.138

Cycle Track

91
7.6

F.W.

F.W.

R.H.

99
1.320

West Row

96
4.666

Eldon

Methodist Chapel
(New Connexion)

97

Hall's Row

Front Row

98a
17.975

Letter Box

School

Double Row

Office Row

98
1.989

F.P.

South Row

Depôt Row

114
4.566

COLLIERY RAILWAY

Coal Depôt

120
2.174

121
2.336

115
3.290

119
2.623

37

Pasture Rows

Public Health

The general population grew rapidly, but the population in the towns grew more rapidly still. The population of Bradford, for example, grew from 4,000 to 106,000 between 1801 and 1861 – an increase of 2,650 per cent in 60 years.

Increases such as these swamped the existing systems for dealing with refuse and sewage. A small village with no sewers may be dirty; a town of a million people with no sewers swims with excrement. Greedy landlords built 'back-to-back' houses, with flimsy walls, no water, no drains and, in some cases, no foundations. Middens (rubbish heaps) collected in the courtyards. There were constant complaints about the lack of privies (toilets). Sewage simply drained into the nearest river; but the river was the only place where poor people could get their water.

Poverty and high rents forced poor people to crowd together. In one house in Glasgow an investigator found several women 'imprisoned under a blanket', because the other members of the family were wearing the household's clothes at that time.

People who lived in such squalor tended to be immoral and violent. Sex and alcohol were their only ways of escaping from the dreadful world in which they existed. Disease flourished in these conditions. There were epidemics of cholera (a disease of the bowels) in 1831-32, 1848-49 and 1865-66. Diseases such as typhus (a disease passed on by lice) and tuberculosis (a disease of the lungs) were endemic – they were present all the time.

Especially for the poor, it was a terrible and tragic time to live.

An unlucky man

'In this house,' said our friend, 'when the scarlet fever was raging in the neighbourhood, the barber who was living here suffered fearfully from it, and no sooner did the man get well of this than he was seized with typhus, and scarcely had he recovered from the first attack of that, than he was struck down a second time with the same terrible disease. Since then he has lost his child from cholera, and at this moment his wife is suffering from the same disease. The only wonder is that they are not all dead; for as the barber sat at his meals in his small shop, if he put up his hand against the wall behind him, it would be covered with the soil of his neighbour's privy, soaking through the wall.'

Henry Mayhew, *London Characters (1874)*

QUESTION

Study the picture opposite. List everything which makes it a place in which you would not want to live.

Right: The Gullet, an alley in Birmingham, in 1876.

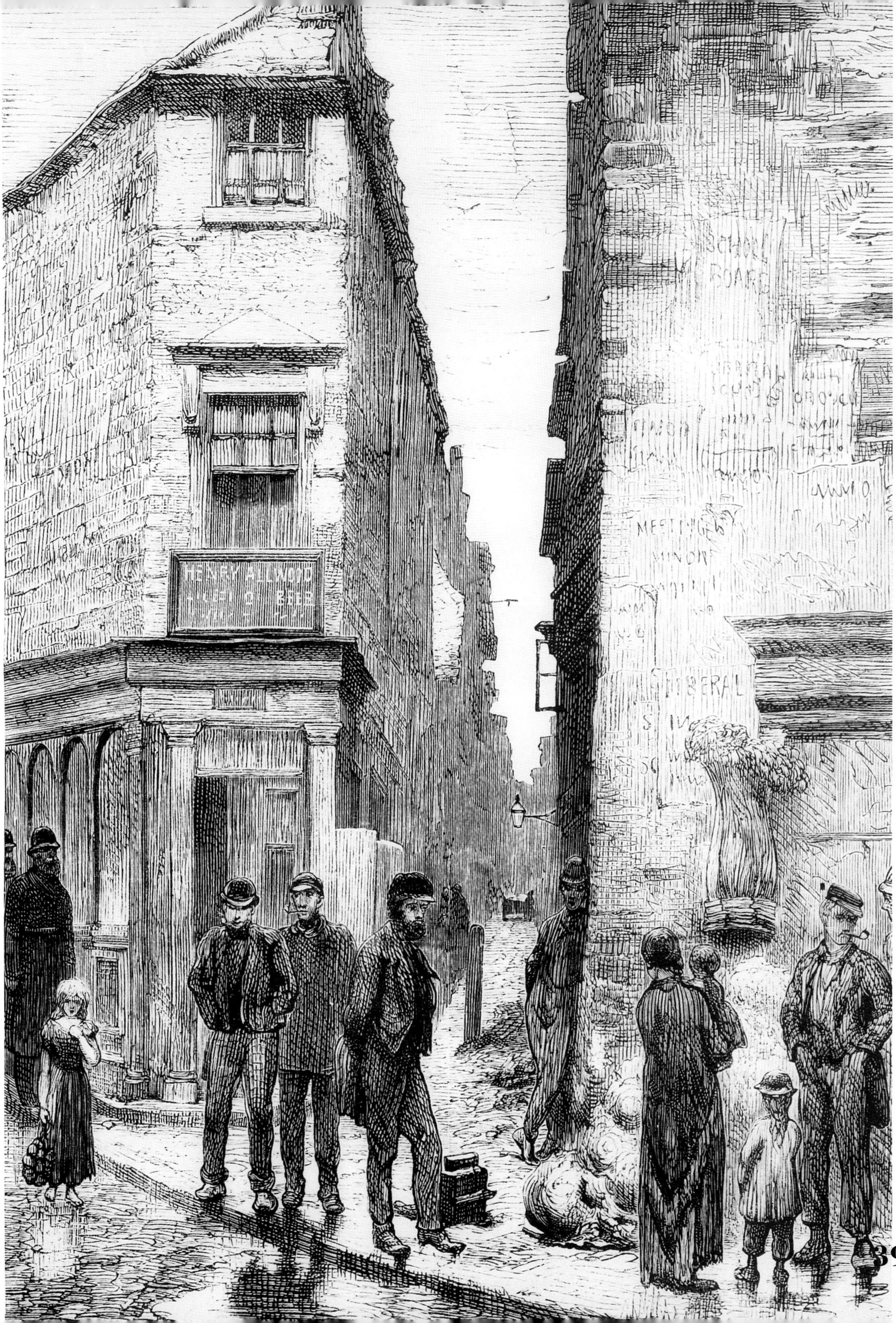

IN THE

In Prison
Three hundred women were crowded together in the two wards.... Here they kept their multitudes of children; and they had no other place for cooking, washing, eating and sleeping. They all slept on the floor without a mat for bedding.
T. Fowell (1818)

RENT: 3p

Clayrow, Darlington
In a room of less than 10 feet square, I found 5 men, 3 women and 3 children, two of whom were covered in smallpox! There was no furniture except two broken chairs.... Near to the fireplace stood a bucket of the most detestable messes, whilst fronting the window was an open dunghill.
Health Board Report (1851)

RENT: 4p

Bradford Canal
The drains of the town empty into this watercourse. Besides, there are a great many factories, the soil, refuse and filth of which fall into the beck. In summertime, the water is low, and all the filth accumulates for weeks, or months, and emits a most offensive smell.
Bradford Surveyors (1844)

RENT: 6p

IN THE GUTTER

Market Street, Greenock
It is too large to be called a dunghill. It contains 100 cubic yards of pure filth; it is the stock-in-trade of a person who sells dung. The smell all round in summer is horrible. Each house swarms with flies; any article of food left out becomes unfit to use, from the strong taste of the dunghill left by the flies.
Parliamentary Report (1842)

RENT: 6p

Glasgow
In the lower lodging-houses, ten, twelve, and sometimes twenty persons of both sexes and all ages sleep promiscuously on the floor in different degrees of nakedness. These places are, as regards dirt, damp and decay, such as no person would stable his horse in.
Hand-Weavers Report (1839)

RENT: 2p

METROPOLY

GO
If you are not in the gutter, collect 20p wages as you pass.

Long Millgate, Manchester
In one of the courts, just at the entrance where the covered passage ends, there is a privy without a door. The privy is so dirty that the inhabitants of the court can only enter or leave the court if they are prepared to wade through puddles of stale urine and excrement.
F. Engels (1844)

RENT: 4p

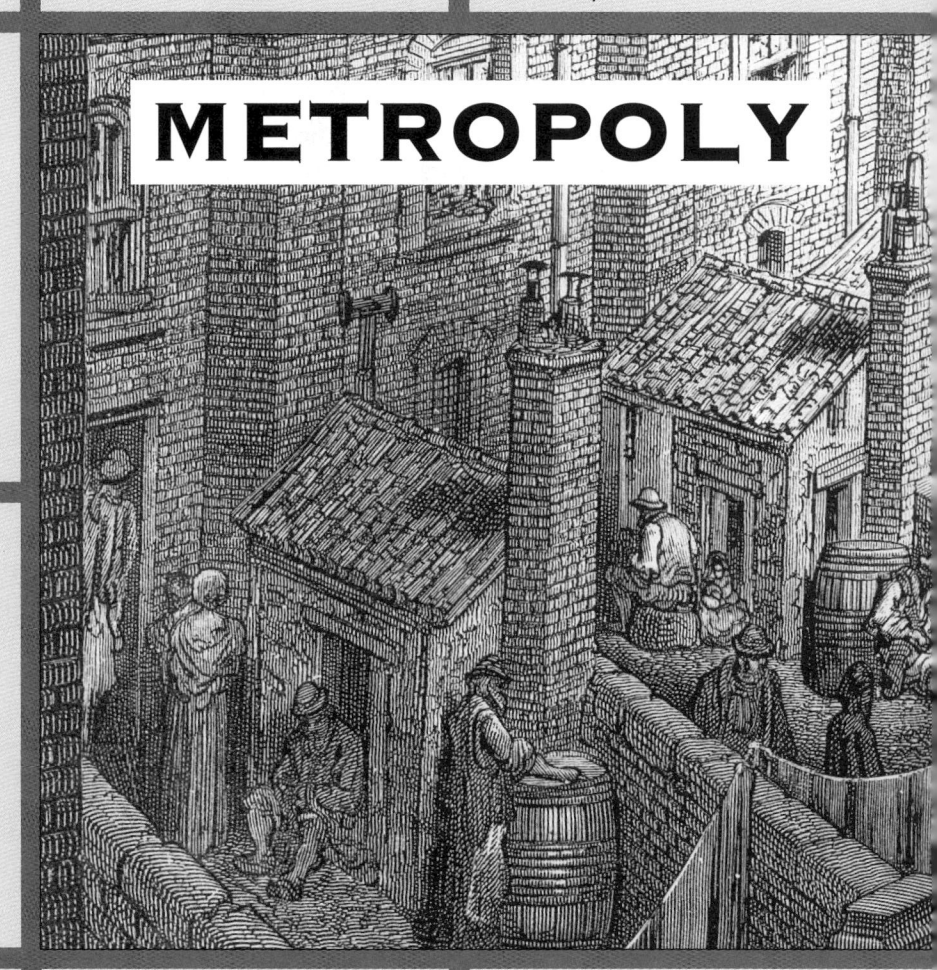

Avon Street, Bath
An epidemic of smallpox carried off upwards of 300 persons, settling mainly on Avon Street. Everything vile and offensive is congregated there. All the scum of Bath – its low prostitutes, its thieves, its beggars – are piled up in the dens of which the street consists.
Parliamentary Report (1842)

RENT: 5p

IN THE

GUTTER

Bradford
Dr Bell, the Bradford Poor Law Doctor, reported that the area housed 1450 people in 230 houses. These people had between them 435 beds and 36 privies, giving averages of 6 persons per house, three per bed and forty per privy.
Poor Law Report (1861)

RENT: 3p

The Back Streets of Leeds
Broken panes in every window frame, and filth and vermin in every nook. With the walls unwhitewashed for years, black with the smoke of foul chimneys, without water . . . and with sacking for bed-clothes, with floors unwashed from year to year, without privies.
Parliamentary Report (1842)

RENT: 3p

FREE LODGINGS

(pick up a CHANCE card)

Model Cottages, Hyde Park
The living room has an area of about 150 feet, with a cupboard on one side of the fireplace. The kitchen is fitted up with a sink. The sleeping rooms, three in number, allow for that separation which, with a family, is so essential to morality and decency. The water closet is fitted up with a glazed basin.
Great Exhibition (1851)

RENT: 20p

IN THE GUTTER

Cheyne Road, London
Its stillness, its panelled walls, its carved banisters, and the quiet garden behind . . . . In the drawing room stood that enchanting screen, covered with pictures; upstairs was the panelled drawing-room with its wonderful view, and the portrait of Oliver Cromwell hanging opposite the windows.
Fuller & Hammersley (1851)

RENT: £15.00

CHANCE

Epping
All drinking-water of the house came from a well beneath the floor of the kitchen; and into that well there was habitual soakage from the water-closet. From the time when Mr and Mrs G. returned home ill, the diarrhoea which passed from their bowels gave an extra and peculiar taste to the already-foul water-supply.
Privy Council Report (1865)

RENT: 7p

Bermondsey, London
We saw drains emptying into it, we saw a row of doorless privies built over it, we heard bucket after bucket of filth splash into it. As we stood gazing in horror at the sewer, we asked if they *really did* drink the water? The answer was, 'They had to drink the water unless they could steal a bucketful of the real Thames.'
H. Mayhew (1874)

RENT: 2p

GO TO PRISON

GUTTER

41

CHANGES IN THE ECONOMY

Economics is the study of the wealth and resources of a country. 'The British economy' is that part of our lives which is to do with making and buying goods and services.

Sometime during the eighteenth century, the British economy began to change. Historians call these developments the Industrial Revolution.

Britain 'invented' the Industrial Revolution, and then gave it to the rest of the world. It is perhaps the most amazing thing the people of Britain have ever done. Yet nobody really knows why – or even exactly when – it started!

This chapter looks at the Industrial Revolution in Britain.

The changes in methods of farming seem so great that some historians have called them the Agricultural Revolution (see pages 43-49). In the first section of this chapter you will be able to study the changes in farming and form your own opinion as to whether there was a 'revolution' in agriculture in the eighteenth century.

Greater changes occurred in industry. Businessmen invested large amounts of money in the textile industry (see pages 52-57), in coal mining (pages 58-65) and in transport (pages 66-71). There were some important inventions. Production increased rapidly. This chapter deals with these changes and how they affected the people of Britain.

QUESTIONS

1 What made businessmen decide to invest their money in industry?
2 Where did the money come from?
Look back at pages 14-15 (the growth of trade) and 34-35 (population). Use the information you discover to suggest answers to these questions.

Farming – Continuity or Change?

Historians study the changes that have taken place over the centuries, but they also have to understand that sometimes things stayed the same (this is called continuity). These pictures of ploughing come from the period 1500 BC – AD 1800.

A

B

C

D

QUESTIONS

1. Try to put the pictures into chronological order (order of date).
2. Why is this exercise so difficult?

Chapter 4

Farming in the Eighteenth Century

In the eighteenth century, much of England was still farmed in the way that it had been in Medieval times. The pictures on this page show scenes typical of farming in about 1750.

PLOUGHING

HARROWING

SOWING

REAPING

THRASHING & WINDING

BAKEHOUSE

??????? QUESTIONS ???????

1. Try to work out what is happening in each picture.
2. The pictures show a progression – they tell the story of how bread was made, from ploughing the land to baking the bread. Explain to a friend how each stage prepared the way for, and led on to, the next picture.

Changes in the Economy

Open Field Farming

In the eighteenth century many English villages had three huge Open Fields, divided into strips. Each farmer owned a number of strips scattered about the three fields. Every year, in turn, one of the great fields would be left fallow (uncultivated) to let it rest. On the other two fields, crops such as wheat or barley would be grown; the villagers would come to an agreement about which crop they would grow in each field.

Other land – the Common – was set aside for the whole community. Villagers had the right to graze a number of animals on the Common, and to collect firewood from it. Occasionally, some people even built houses there (though they had no right to do so; they were called 'squatters').

Open Field farming had lots of problems (see right). It provided enough food for the villagers ('subsistence farming'), but it did not create a surplus to feed the inhabitants of the growing towns.

The problems of Open Fields

1 Farmers wasted time travelling from one strip to another.

2 It was impossible to use modern machinery on the small, awkwardly-shaped strips.

3 Weeds from bad farmers' land spread easily to other strips.

4 Little fodder (animal food) was produced, so many animals had to be killed before the winter.

5 Because everyone grew the same thing, farmers were unable to experiment with new crops.

6 Land was wasted – e.g. paths between strips; the fallow field.

7 All the farmers' animals grazed together on the Common, so disease spread easily.

8 On the Common, good animals bred with poor-quality animals.

A plan of an imaginary Open Field village, showing the strips owned by a poor farmer (K) and the Lord of the Manor (A).

Chapter 4

The Agricultural Revolution

If you have read any other school textbooks about the Agricultural Revolution, you will probably have read an account which goes more or less like this:

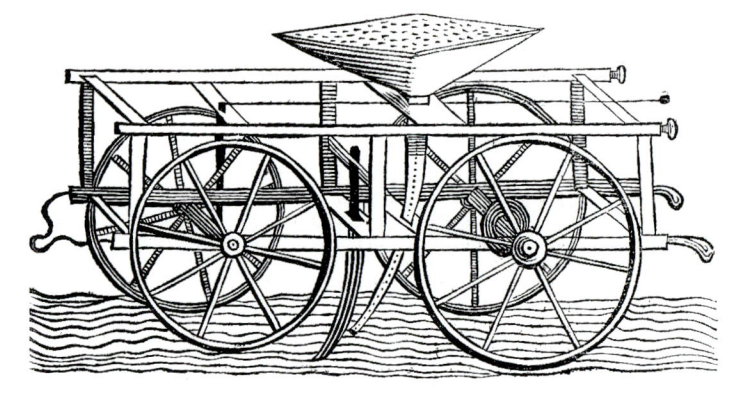

1 An early seed drill.

New ways of farming

Farmers began to use machinery. In 1701 **Jethro Tull** invented a **seed-drill** [picture 1]. It sowed the seeds in rows under the soil, so farmers could abandon the old, wasteful way of sowing broadcast (by hand). Later, Tull invented a horse-hoe to weed the crops. Other **farm machinery** was invented, including threshing and winnowing machines, and a reaping machine (in 1826). In 1856 John Fowler of Leeds invented a **steam plough**.

New methods of growing crops were introduced. **'Turnip' Townshend**, from Norfolk, developed the **Norfolk Four-Course** rotation. This was a four-year crop rotation, with wheat, turnips, barley and clover being planted in turn. No land was wasted, because no land was left fallow. **Clover** and **turnips** [picture 2] are fodder crops, which could be fed to the animals during the winter months. This meant that the animals could put on more weight and give more meat.

Improvements were also made in animal breeding. **Robert Bakewell** from Leicestershire produced better animals by making sure that only the best animals were used for breeding [picture 3]. This is called selective breeding. Bakewell rented out his rams to other farmers, so they too could breed better animals.

These new methods of farming could not be practised on the old Open Fields, so large areas of land were **enclosed**. Millions of acres were fenced in. Farming became more efficient.

2 Right: Turnips and clover.

3 Left: Robert Bakewell bred a new variety of sheep called the New Leicesters.

46

Changes in the Economy

Enclosure

During the eighteenth century, many villages applied to Parliament for an Act of Enclosure (see right). Men called Enclosure Commissioners were appointed, who re-drew the map of the village, putting each landowner's land together into one farm. The landowners could then divide up their farm into fields as they wanted.

The Commissioners swore an oath:

I do swear that I will faithfully, fairly and honestly, according to the best of my skill, [divide the land] without favour or affection to any persons whatsoever.

Do you believe it? Until recently, many historians did not. They thought that the Commissioners helped the rich landowners to swindle the poor out of their land. Modern historians, however, believe that the Commissioners WERE fair.

The problem with enclosure was that, even though it was fair and legal, it still damaged the poor farmers. People lost their land if they did not have documents which proved their legal right to their land. Squatters were turned off the Common. Most of all, the high cost of getting the Act, paying the Commissioner and fencing the land after the enclosure usually ruined poor farmers. They had to sell their new farms to the rich landowners.

Applying for an Act of Enclosure

1 The owners of four-fifths of the land met and agreed to ask Parliament for an Act of Enclosure.
Sometimes the Lord of the Manor alone owned four-fifths of the land.

2 Parliament passed the Act, agreeing to enclose the village land.
Remember that at this time all MPs were rich landowners and merchants.

3 A Commissioner was appointed to draw up the enclosure.
Often he stayed at the house of the local Lord of the Manor.

4 A notice was pinned to the church door, telling the villagers that there was going to be an enclosure.
Sometimes, this was the first that some villagers had heard about the enclosure.

5 The Commissioners drew up an Enclosure Award, based on how much land each farmer owned.
The villagers could dispute the Award, but all claims had to be made in writing, and supported by legal documents.

6 The final Award was stored in the local church.
Farmers had six months to fence or hedge their land, or lose it.

??? QUESTION ???

Look at the six stages of enclosure (above). In what different ways were poor farmers at a disadvantage?

Challenge!

The only problem with the description of the Agricultural Revolution on pages 46–47 is that it may be wrong! The facts on these pages will allow you to challenge the traditional view that there was an 'Agricultural Revolution'.

1 Ploughing, using oxen. Use the information on page 44 to guess the date of this photograph.

2 Jethro Tull was an eccentric man. He invented the horse-hoe, not to weed the crops, but because he thought that plants grew by absorbing the soil. He broke up the soil so that the roots could absorb it more easily.

3 The real agricultural revolution in farm machinery came after 1945, when farmers began to use tractors in large numbers.

4 Bakewell charged so much for his rams that ordinary farmers could not afford them. For many years 'selective breeding' was just a rich man's hobby.

5 'Turnip' Townshend was a failed politician. He got his nickname more as a political joke (when he had to go home to his country estate) than because of his farming achievements.

Changes in the Economy

6 Only a quarter of the farmland in England and Wales was enclosed by Act of Parliament during the 18th century. Most of England had already been enclosed long before 1750.

7 Few farmers outside Norfolk used the Norfolk Four-Course rotation. Most farmers rested their land by sowing it with grass and putting animals out to graze (which manured the land).

8 Turnips were of limited importance. They cannot be grown on acid soil or on heavy soils. Turnips rot in wet soil, and they are easily killed by frost.

9 Clover was brought over from Holland, not after 1750, but after 1688. It was well known by the time of 'Turnip' Townshend.

10 Sowing broadcast. Use the information on page 44 to guess the date of this photograph.

QUESTIONS

1 Photograph 1 was taken in 1957. Photograph 10 was taken in 1941. Why is this surprising?
2 Make a list of all the words in bold type on page 46. They are the key words in the traditional way of looking at the Agricultural Revolution. For each, find a fact (1-10) which contradicts it.
3 Do facts 1-10 prove that there was not an Agricultural Revolution at all?
4 Look back at pages 34-35. What is the strongest argument that there was some kind of Agricultural Revolution in Britain in the eighteenth century?

49

Chapter 4

The Village of the Living Dead

In Ireland, the population grew as quickly as it did in England, but in Ireland there were no agricultural changes to produce more food for its growing population. By the middle of the nineteenth century, many Irish people were living on nothing but potatoes and milk – and in 1845, the potato crop failed. A potato blight turned the potatoes into a black, foul-smelling mush . . . with tragic consequences.

22 December, 1846

My Lord Duke,

I went on the 15th to the village of Skibbereen in southern Ireland. I shall state simply what I saw there.

On reaching the spot I was surprised to find the wretched village apparently deserted. I entered some of the hovels to find out why. The scenes which I saw were such as no tongue or pen can give the slightest idea.

In the first hut, six famished and ghastly skeletons, to all appearances dead, were huddled in a corner on some filthy straw. Their only covering was what seemed to be a ragged horsecloth. I went closer with horror, and found by a low moaning that they were alive. They were ill with fever; four children, a woman and what had once been a man.

It is impossible to tell the whole story. I shall only say that in a few minutes I was surrounded by at least 200 such phantoms, such frightful ghosts as no words can describe, victims either of famine or of fever. Their demoniac yells are still ringing in my ears, and their horrible faces are fixed upon my brain. My heart sickens when I write about it, but I must go on.

My clothes were nearly torn off as I tried to escape from the crowd of sick people all around. Then my scarf was grabbed from behind by a grip which forced me to turn. I found myself held by a woman with a new-born baby in her arms and the remains of a filthy sack round her waist. This was all she had to cover herself and the baby.

On the same morning the police opened a house in the fields nearby, which was noticed shut for many days, and two frozen corpses were found, lying upon the mud floor, eaten by rats.

I am sir, etc.
Nicholas Cummins, J.P.

Changes in the Economy

The Irish Famine

The Irish potato crop failed again in 1846, 1847 and 1848. The British government did little to help. People starved to death. Disease followed famine. A third of the population of Ireland died. Thousands more emigrated to America.

These drawings date from around the time of the famine.

Chapter 4

The Textile Industry

1 Spinning by hand. The 'spinster' holds the roving (a thick band of combed wool) in her left hand. The roving is attached to the spindle. She pulls it out, to make the yarn (thread) thinner. At the same time, she turns the large 'muckle wheel', which turns the spindle, which twists the yarn.

It took two or three spinners to supply yarn for one weaver. The yarn was thick and weak.

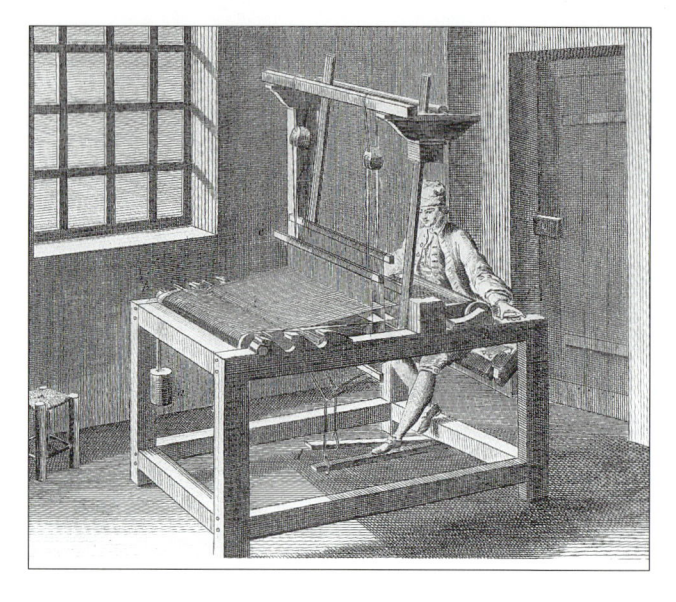

2 An eighteenth-century hand-loom weaver. A foot pedal raises every other warp thread to create the 'shed' (gap). In his left hand he holds the shuttle, which carries the weft thread. He passes the shuttle through the shed. The maximum width of cloth is 70 centimetres (a 'shortcloth'). To make wider cloth there had to be two weavers, to throw the shuttle back and forth.

In the eighteenth century, cloth was made by hand in the workers' own homes (see pictures 1 and 2).

Then, in 1733, John Kay of Bury invented a weaving machine called the flying shuttle. He put the shuttle on wheels, so weavers could knock it backwards and forwards with a simple mechanism called a picker. This allowed wider cloth to be made, more quickly. The spinners could not keep up. There was a need for an invention which would speed up spinning. In fact, three machines were invented.

In about 1764, James Hargreaves of Blackburn invented the 'spinning jenny' (see picture 3). This allowed the spinner to spin many threads at the same time, although the yarn was not as strong as that produced by hand spinners.

Soon after, in about 1769, a better spinning machine was invented by Richard Arkwright of Preston (although some people say he stole the idea from his partner). Arkwright's machine produced a strong, thick thread (see diagram 4).

3 The spinning jenny. The wheel has been adapted so that it turns 16 spindles. A clamp is placed on a moving carriage which allows the spinner to pull out all the threads at once.

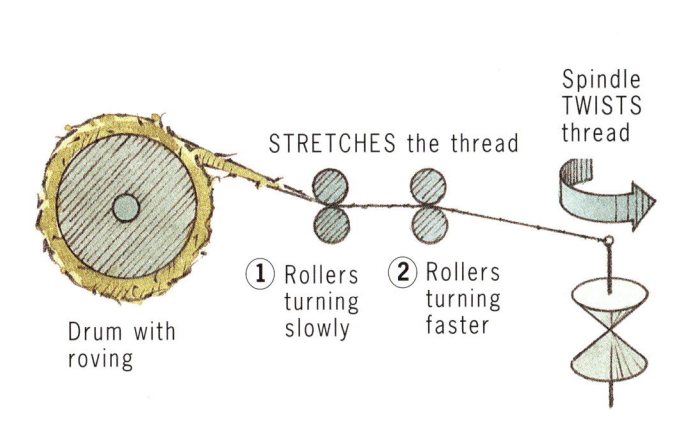

4 How Arkwright's 'frame' worked. Rollers 1 turn more slowly than rollers 2, which stretches the roving in between. A spindle twists the yarn. This large machine needed a water wheel to power it, and became known as the 'water frame'.

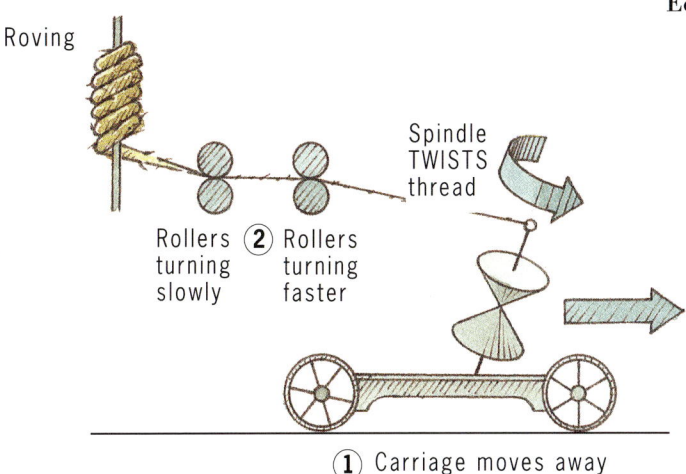

5 To stretch the roving, Crompton used both Hargreaves' idea of a moving carriage (1) and Arkwright's idea of rollers (2). His machine was therefore nicknamed the 'mule' (a mule is a cross between a horse and a donkey).

In 1779, Samuel Crompton of Bolton invented a machine which spun thread that was finer and stronger than anything the hand-spinners could make (see diagram 5). The introduction of machinery was helped by the development of the steam engine. Thomas Newcomen had invented a simple steam engine in 1712, which had been used to drain the coal mines. In 1765 James Watt improved Newcomen's design, and in 1781 he invented the 'sun and planet gear', an invention which turned the up-and-down motion of the steam engine into rotary (round and round) motion. This meant that steam engines could now be used to power machinery in factories.

Every employer bought the new machines. Spinning became mechanised. By 1812 one spinner operating a machine in a factory could make as much as 200 domestic spinsters could have made 50 years earlier. Production of yarn increased greatly.

At first, this glut of yarn was good for the hand-loom weavers who wove the yarn. They had so much work, they could charge what they wanted! Their income grew.

The hand-loom weavers could not weave all the thread being made by the spinning machines; there was clearly a need for a weaving invention. In 1785 Edmund Cartwright, a vicar from Leicestershire, invented a power-loom. By 1800 the design had been improved and businessmen began to use these looms in their factories. By 1850 weaving, too, was fully mechanised.

The invention of the power-loom was disastrous for the hand-loom weavers. They could not keep up with the power-looms. They could not even get a job in a factory, because the new power-looms could be worked by women and children, who were paid much less than the men. So the hand-loom weavers became very poor and overworked as they struggled to work as fast as the new machines. They failed.

Production in the wool and cotton industries grew rapidly. But this increase would have been no use if the manufacturers had not been able to sell the extra cloth they made. The spinning and weaving inventions did not CAUSE the revolution in textiles, they ALLOWED it to happen.

Foul Factories

In the eighteenth century most people had worked in their own homes (the 'domestic system'). The textile revolution changed this.

Businessmen built factories. This was partly because the new machines were too large to fit into people's homes and needed a steam engine to power them. Another reason was that factories gave the businessmen greater control over how and when people worked. The main reason, however, was that ordinary people could not afford to buy the new machines, so the industry came to be controlled by a few very wealthy businessmen.

Many history books tell you that the factories were dreadful places. For example:

A nineteenth century factory

To help stop the cotton threads from snapping, the inside of the cotton factories was kept very hot and very moist . . . . This noisy, steamy atmosphere was thick with dust and fluff from the cotton . . . . It is not surprising that the death rate from tuberculosis and lung diseases was horrifying.

Twelve to fourteen hours a day from Monday to Saturday with a 'short' day of four hours to clean the machinery on Sunday was quite usual, even for small children . . . no one, not even small children, was allowed to sit down . . . . Even during the short breakfast and tea breaks many factories kept their engines running . . . . Small children, who often had to bend their bodies into unnatural positions to do their jobs properly, frequently grew up with twisted spines, crooked thighs and knock-knees. Finally . . . there were always the machines themselves waiting to mangle workers who became caught in them . . . .

At the beginning of the century there were no laws at all about the age at which boys and girls could start work . . . . While floggings and beatings were bad enough, it was the injustice of the harsh fines that hurt the adult workers most of all . . . . the overlookers were threatened with dismissal if they did not collect enough fines or get an almost impossible amount of work done. Sometimes the overlookers seemed to delight in inflicting savage punishments on the women and children . . . .

Adapted from **Peter Moss**, History Alive III (1968)

Educated Victorians who visited the factories were horrified. In 1831-32 hundreds of people who worked in the mills were interviewed by a Commission of Parliament. These are some of things they said:

1 Robert Blincoe, once an apprentice in a cotton-mill:

Have you had any accidents from the machinery? – I have not myself, but I saw a man killed by machinery at Stockport; he was smashed, and he died in four or five hours . . . he was accidentally drawn up by the drive-belt, and was killed.

2 Joseph Badder, an overlooker:

I have often had complaints against myself by the parents of children for beating them. I used to beat them. I am sure that no man can do without it who works long hours. I told them I was very sorry after I had done it, but I was forced to it. The master expected me to do my work, and I could not do mine unless they did theirs.

3 James Carpenter, Leeds millhand:

What means were taken to keep the children to their work? – Sometimes they would tap them over the head, or nip them over the nose, or throw water in their faces, or shake them about to keep them awake.

4 Mark Best, an overlooker:

Were the children fined as well as beaten sometimes? – Yes. For various things; if they were caught combing their hair before they went home, or washing themselves . . . they would not even allow them to speak to one another.

5 Samuel Downe, aged 29; a factory worker living near Leeds:

At the age of about ten I began work at Mr Marshall's mill at Shrewsbury, where the usual hours of work when work was brisk were generally 5 a.m. to 8 p.m.

6 Joseph Hebergam; he had worked since he was seven:

When I had worked about half a year, a weakness fell into my knees and ankles. In the morning I could scarcely walk, and my brother and sister used out of kindness to take me under each arm, and run with me, a good mile, to the mill, and my legs dragged on the ground because of the pain; I could not walk. If we were five minutes too late, the overlooker would take a strap, and beat us till we were black and blue.

7 Charles Burn, aged 14; he began work at the age of eight:

How often were you allowed to go to the toilet? – Three times a day. *Were you allowed to go to the toilet at any time you wanted?* – No; only when a boy came to tell you it was your turn.

8 Elizabeth Bentley, aged 23; she began work at the age of six:

Did it affect your health? – Yes; it was so dusty, the dust got upon my lungs . . . . I got so bad in health, that when I pulled the baskets down, I pulled my bones out of their places.

Foul Factories?

Modern historians have read what the Victorians wrote, and assumed that conditions in the factories really were terrible. But were Victorian factories really so bad? The sources on these pages will help you to make up your own mind.

1 Samuel Coulson of Leeds

Coulson's children worked in a mill. Here, he answers questions about the work his children did in the 'brisk' times (when the mill was busy):

At what time in the morning, in the brisk time, did these girls go to the mills? – In the brisk time, for about six weeks, they have gone at 3 o'clock in the morning, and ended at 10, or nearly half past, at night.
  What breaks were allowed for rest during those nineteen hours of work? – Breakfast a quarter of an hour, and dinner half an hour, and drinking a quarter of an hour.
  What was the length of time they could be in bed during those long hours? – It was near 11 o'clock before we could get them into bed after getting a little food, [then] me or my mistress got up at 2 o'clock to dress them.
  Were the children excessively tired by this work? – Many a time; we have cried often when we have given them the little food we had to give them; we had to shake them and they have fallen to sleep with the food in their mouth.

Evidence given to the Commission of Parliament (1831-32).

2 John Wood of Bradford

John Wood was a mill-owner who spent his life trying to improve factory conditions. Here William Sharp, a doctor, describes Wood's mill:

Has anything struck you about the mills? – That they were particularly cleanly, and made as comfortable as they can be . . . .
  Has Mr Wood baths upon his premises? – Yes.
  Do you happen to know whether seats are provided? – There are seats.
  Will you state the number of hours they are employed? – From 6 a.m. to 7 p.m., with half an hour for breakfast and forty minutes for dinner.

Evidence given to the Commission of Parliament (1831-32).

In 1833, a reporter from *Penny Magazine* visited Wood's factory. He wrote an article to show how happy the workers were:

It was the hour for dinner and play, and the young people were joyfully sporting in the open yard of the factory . . . . All seemed glad to see him . . . . The little people seemed quite delighted to see their employer; their faces brightened up and their eyes sparkled as he came near; indeed, he appeared more like a father among them, and an affectionate one too, than like a master.

Penny Magazine (1833)

Can You Believe Your Eyes?

3 *Below*: This picture was drawn in about 1835 for a book called *The Progress of Cotton*. The book was written to teach children in other countries about cotton manufacturing in Britain.

The picture shows spinning mules. Notice the child sweeping up the cotton dust under the machine, and the woman 'piecener' mending broken threads.

5 *Above*: The same picture, adapted yet again for a book by John Cobden, *The White Slaves of England*, written in 1860. The book was designed to win public support for the campaign to improve conditions in the factories.

4 *Above*: The same scene, adapted for Frances Trollope's book, *Michael Armstrong, Factory Boy* – a tear-jerker of a novel about the tragic life of a young orphan, written in 1840.

??? QUESTIONS ???

1. Which of the sources suggest that conditions were bad in the factories? Which suggest that conditions were good?
2. Look again at sources 1 and 2. Which do you believe? Explain your reasoning.
3. Look again at pictures 4 and 5. Explain how in each the artist has adapted picture 3 to make it show the kind of scene he wanted.
4. Which picture, do you think, gives the most reliable evidence of what factories were like? What kind of conditions does this picture show?

Coal Mining

The Death Pit

It was the afternoon of 16 February, 1909, in the mining town of Stanley, in County Durham. At the town's mine, Ralph Stephenson, the engineer, heard a dull rumble. He walked over to the pit mouth and looked down into the shaft.

Burns Pit, named after its owner, had four seams of coal. The Towneley seam was 225 metres underground. Below it were the Tilley and the Busty seams. The Brockwell was the lowest, 300 metres deep. In the Brockwell seam, a pocket of methane gas – called 'firedamp' by the miners – had been ignited by a Howart's safety lamp. There was a small explosion.

Below ground, the miners heard the bang. Richard Proud, aged 14, took cover in a manhole. He knew what would happen next. Through the mine a rush of air whipped up the coal dust. The dust of any combustible material – even custard powder – becomes explosive when the specks are surrounded by air, and coal dust is especially dangerous.

At the surface, Ralph Stephenson heard the pit growl. He saw a red glow at the bottom of the shaft. Fifty seconds after the first explosion, the coal dust ignited. A huge fireball rushed up the shaft and burst past Stephenson, rising high into the air; then, mysteriously, it reversed and sucked the smoke and flames back down into the mine.

Underground, dozens of miners had been killed. Richard Proud was dead. William Chaytor, 55, had also been killed. His watch had stopped at 3.45 p.m., the time of the explosion. One man's head had been smashed open; they found his brains far away by a pit-prop. A young boy and his pony had been moving tubs of coal when the blast struck. They found his body under the pony; his head was beneath one of the tubs.

Life in the town stopped in its tracks. A terrible wail went up as the women realised what had happened. Then everybody ran to the mine. In the rush, Fitz Armstrong, the son of the local postmaster, was knocked down and killed by a horse-bus.

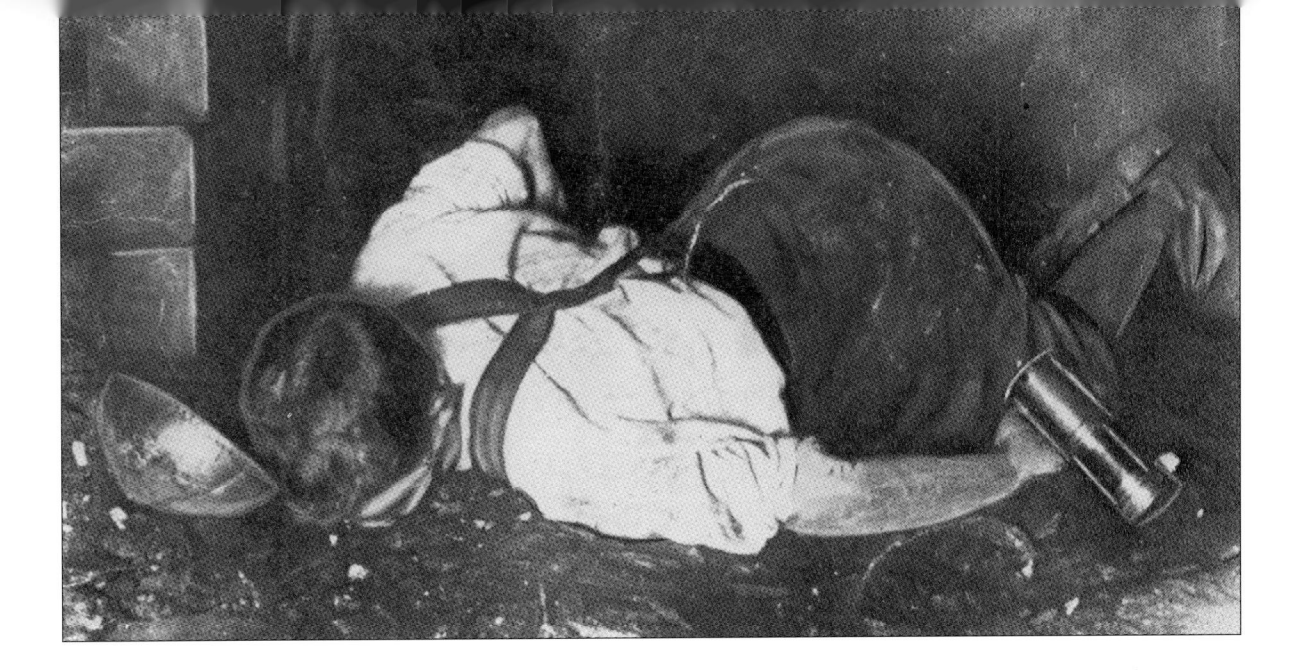

For hours nothing could be done. The manager was away seeking another job. Rescue equipment had to be fetched from a nearby mine. Nobody knew who was underground, or even how many men were down there.

One weeping girl caught the attention of a kindly miner. 'What's the matter, hinny?' he asked. Her mother had died some time before, and her father and two brothers were in the mine. The Reverend Watson knelt with her and prayed and cried.

Some miners had survived both blasts, but explosions are not the end in a mine disaster. After the two explosions, 'chokedamp' (carbon monoxide) swept through the mine, suffocating many of the survivors. They lay life-like, their eyes open, their faces flushed pink with the effects of the gas.

Even so, some men were still alive in the Tilley seam, which had avoided the worst of the blast. One of them was Mark Henderson, a deputy. He gathered 36 men together and took them to a small gallery where there was some fresh air left.

There, they waited. Hours passed. Two men panicked and rushed off into the mine. Soon after, seven more followed; they found them later, suffocated by the chokedamp.

Someone began to sing a hymn:

Lead kindly light,
    amid the encircling gloom,
    Lead Thou me on;
The night is dark,
    and I am far from home,
    Lead Thou me on . . . .

The miners joined in. One of them, Bob Harrison, was in the Salvation Army. Yet even as they sang, little Jimmy Garner, 14, his legs crushed, lay back and died.

Henderson realised that he would have to go for help. Covering his mouth against the gases and choking smoke, he made his way along the passages to the only working telephone: 'Can you get us out?' It took 14 hours to rescue the men.

Some good did come from the disaster; mines started to use a system of tallies so they could always know how many men were underground. But the loss was terrible. Only 30 men survived. One hundred and sixty-eight men died; 60 of them were under the age of 20.

Burns Pit finally closed down in 1936. The people of Stanley hated it. One night, the watchman went over to the old shaft. 'Damn you!' he shouted down.

In the emptiness, his voice echoed back to him. 'Damn you,' replied Burns Pit.

Chapter 4

King Coal

Coal had been used before the Industrial Revolution, for fires, and in the brewing, pottery and glass industries.

All this changed in the years after 1750. The Industrial Revolution was based on coal more than anything else (see source 1). Vast amounts of coal were needed.

Unlike other industries, however, there were no great inventions which revolutionised the production of coal. Mine owners simply used the same techniques, and dug deeper mines (see source 2).

As they dug deeper, accidents and explosions became more frequent.

To try to stop deaths from firedamp, Humphrey Davy invented a safety lamp in 1815. A wire gauze stopped the gas getting to the flame. But the Davy lamp did not save lives. It merely allowed the owners to mine more 'fiery' seams of coal, and so the deaths continued.

1 The wonders of coal

- Coal was used as fuel for steam engines.
- In 1709, Abraham Darby discovered how to use coal to make iron.
- Coal was used to heat houses.
- After 1830, coal was used to make coal gas (for heating and lighting).
- After 1859, coal was used to make dyes (first to be discovered was the red dye, magenta).
- Coal was the basis of fertilisers, ink, perfumes, sulphuric acid, explosives, pesticides and paint.
- Ammonia, another by-product of coal, was used as a disinfectant. In the First World War, it was used as a poison gas.
- After 1872, doctors used coal-based dyes in their research into germs.

After the period 1750-1914:
- After 1935, coal was the basis of the 'sulphonamide' drugs which cured blood-poisoning.
- Later still, coal was the basis of research into plastics and nylon.

2 Coal production in the U.K.

Year	Coal output	No. of miners
1701	not known	
1761	5,000,000	16,000
1801	13,000,000	40,000
1861	89,000,000	300,000
1901	229,000,000	950,000

From **Chris Culpin**, *Expansion, Trade and Industry* (1993)

Changes in the Economy

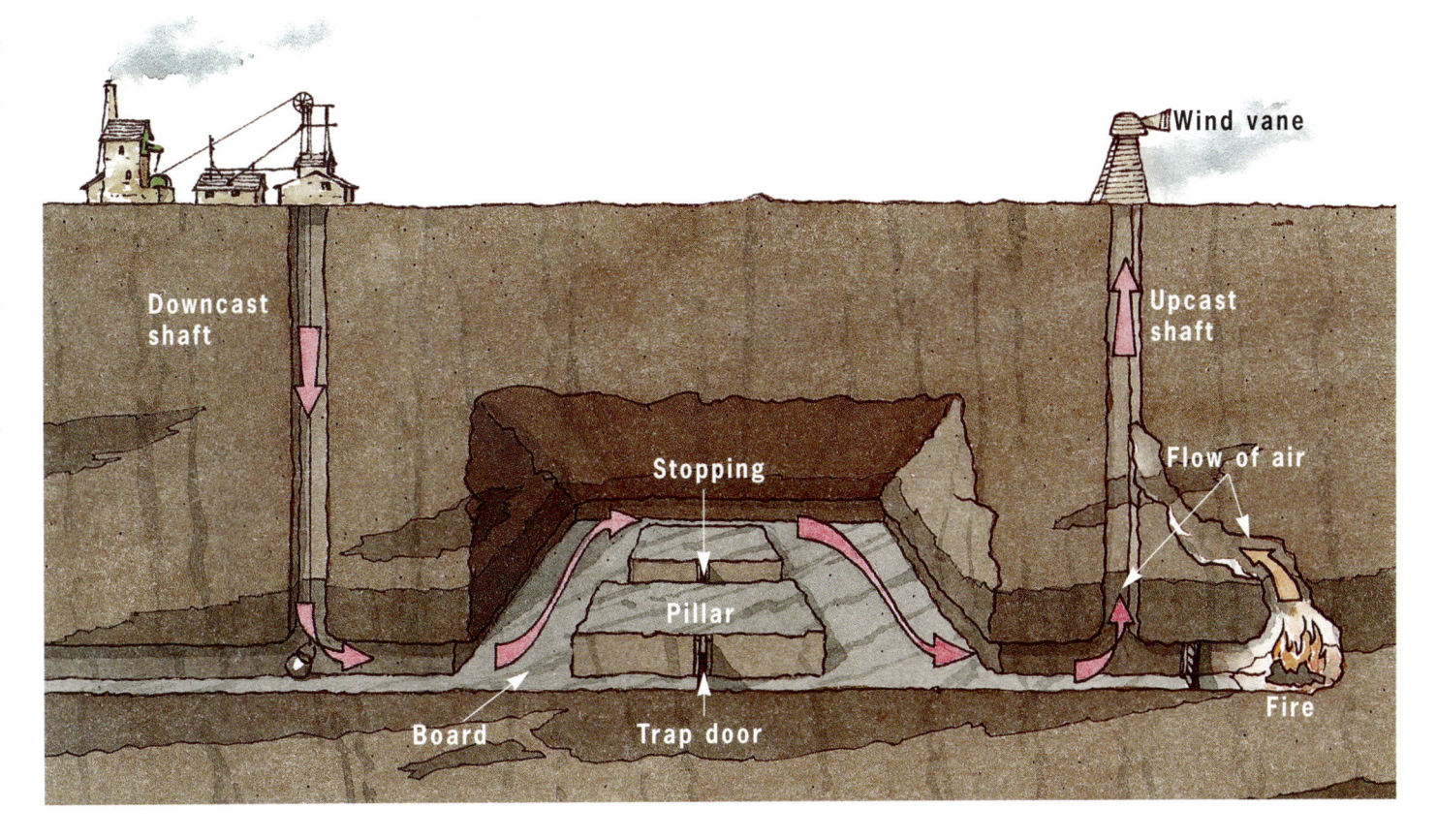

Below: Most mines before 1750 were drift mines (*left*), or shallow bell pits (*right*).

During the Industrial Revolution coal mines were worked by the 'board and pillar' method. Long tunnels – called boards – were cut out of the coal seam, leaving pillars of coal to hold up the roof. The main shaft – which the miners went up and down and the coal came up – was called the downcast shaft. To try to prevent explosions, mine owners ventilated the mines by digging a second shaft – called the upcast shaft. At the bottom of the upcast was a large fire, and the hot air rising from the fire pulled air down the downcast shaft and through the workings.

Walls called stoppings were built to force the air to travel through all the mine workings. If trucks needed to pass along a board where there was a stopping, a door was built, and a child was employed to keep the door shut, opening it only when the coal trucks went through.

61

At the Pit-head

1 Harrington Mill Pit Colliery in Northumberland, c. 1770

A typical late-18th-century colliery. Point out:

- the shaft into the ground (labelled A);
- the winding gear, used to lower miners down the shaft;
- the whim-gin – the horse wheel that was in earlier days used to lower the miners down the shaft;
- the steam engine house, where a new steam engine powered the winding machinery which lowered the miners into the pit and brought up the coal;
- the steam engine's copper boiler behind the house;
- the pile of coal in the foreground;
- a basket used to bring coal up the shaft;
- the loading platform, where the coal was sorted into sizes and loaded onto packhorses.

??? QUESTION ???

Describe in words how coal mines changed between 1770 and 1844.

2 Hebburn Colliery in County Durham, *c.* 1844

A typical 19th-century colliery. Point out:
- the downcast shaft, with corves (coal tubs) being drawn out of the mine;
- the winding gear, used to lower miners down the shaft and to bring up the coal corves;
- the steam engine house, with its chimney, where a steam engine was used to power the winding gear;
- the upcast shaft, with a wind-vane to turn the chimney opening away from the wind at all times;
- the screening sheds, where the coal was sorted into different sizes;
- the railway, on which the coal was taken away to be sold. Note the distinctive chaldron wagons

Chapter 4

The Curse of Coal

In 1840-42, a Royal Commission investigated working conditions in the mines. It was the first report to contain pictures.

1 A woman hurrying (pulling) coal, using a belt and chain.

2 In the larger tunnels, young men called drivers looked after pit ponies, who pulled the trolleys.

3 A girl miner. Investigators were horrified that they dressed like boys.

4 Ann Ambler winching up child workers 'cross-lapped'.

5 Two putters (pushers) thrust the rolleys (tubs on wheels) through the trap-door which the young trapper is opening for them.

6 A hewer cutting coal with a pickaxe.

Changes in the Economy

The 1842 Report

The evidence for the 1842 Report was collected by professional investigators who interviewed mine workers. It led to the Mines Act of 1842, which made it illegal to employ women, and children under ten years of age, in the mines.

But how reliable was the Report?

Sarah Gooder, aged 8:

I'm a trapper in the Gauber pit.

It does not tire me, but I have to trap without a light, and I'm scared.

Sometimes I sing when I have a light, but not in the dark; I dare not sing then.

I don't like being in the pit.

I go to Sunday-schools and read Reading made Easy.

I have heard tell of Jesus many a time.

I don't know why he came to earth, I'm sure, and I don't know why he died, but he had stones for his head to rest on.

I would like to be at school far better than in the pit.

Royal Commission on Employment in the Mines, 1842

Lord Londonderry, a mine owner:

The way [the inspectors] collected their evidence – talking to artful boys and ignorant young girls, and asking questions which in many cases seemed to suggest the answer, was anything but fair . . . . The trapper's work is neither cheerless nor dull; nor is he kept in loneliness and darkness . . . . seldom more than five minutes passes without some person passing through his door, and having a word.

The trapper is generally cheerful and contented, and to be found, like other children of his age, occupied with some childish amusement – such as cutting sticks.

Lord Londonderry, *speaking in the House of Lords, 24 June 1842.*

??? QUESTIONS ???

1. Mine owners such as Lord Londonderry were outraged by the inclusion of pictures in the 1842 Report. Suggest reasons for his anger.
2. Read Sarah Gooder's evidence again. Work out what questions the Commissioners asked her.
3. Read the first paragraph of Lord Londonderry's comments. Now you have looked at Sarah Gooder's evidence, do you think Lord Londonderry was right?

Chapter 4

Transport

By coach (*right*). After 1750 private companies called Turnpike Trusts were set up. They charged travellers a 'toll' for travelling on the road, and used the income to improve the road surface.

By canal (*left*). Most British canals were built between 1760 and 1800. This barge is being pulled by the horse on the towpath. Canals needed complicated systems of locks for barges to be able to go up and down hills.

By rail (*left*). This picture is from the middle of the nineteenth century.

The Railways

James Watt had discovered how to turn the up-and-down movement of a steam engine's piston into rotary movement (see page 53). It was only a matter of time before someone put wheels on a steam engine and got it to move by itself.

Richard Trevithick built the first locomotive, which he called the *Racing Steam Horse*. In 1808, he took it to London, put it on a circular track with a high fence round it, and charged people 5p to see it.

In the collieries of the north of England, engineers such as George Stephenson developed the idea. In 1825 he completed the Stockton and Darlington Railway, the world's first steam-hauled public railway. Further improvements followed. Railway mania (a craze for building railways) swept the country in the 1840s. In 1830, only 70 miles of railway line existed; by 1870, in Britain, 423 million passengers travelled on 16,000 miles of line.

QUESTION

Look at the three pictures opposite. For each form of transport, list its advantages and disadvantages.

Ten benefits of the railways

1 Speed of transport.
In 1700 it took four days to get from London to Manchester; in 1880 it took four and a quarter hours. The world 'shrank'. Food (especially milk and fish) got to market faster – and fresher.

2 Speed of communications.
Letters arrived much quicker on the mail trains. The speed at which business was done increased, so the economy could grow more quickly.

3 Cost of transporting goods.
It was cheaper to carry goods on the railways than on canals or roads.

4 Weight of freight.
A horse could pull half a ton. Trains could pull hundreds of tons. Industries such as coal and iron could never have grown without freight trains.

5 Wages.
In 1847, around 257,000 employees worked on the railways. Their wages helped the economy grow.

6 Railway demand.
The railways needed bricks, stone, cement, wooden sleepers, iron and coal in vast quantities; these industries grew. The engineering industry grew up to make the precision parts needed. The telegraph was invented to help communication and safety on the railways.

7 Passenger transport.
In 1844, a new law required every railway company to provide cheap train fares. For the first time, poor people could afford to go to the seaside.

8 Finance.
Money was needed to build the railways (£44 million in 1847). This led to the development of stock exchanges (where shares are sold).

9 Time.
In 1800, every village kept its own time. Noon in Bristol was half an hour after noon in London. After 1880, 'railway time' established a common standard time across Britain.

10 Public Health.
Many of the worst slums were knocked down to build the railway lines and the stations in the cities.

Chapter 4

The Navvies

The men who built the railways were called navigators, or navvies for short. In 1847, a quarter of a million navvies were employed. Their work was dangerous and difficult, but they were exploited by the railway companies, who paid them poorly and treated them badly.

The navvies were famous for drinking and fighting. Wherever they worked, they left pregnant girls behind them. They were so wild that in 1870 a special mission was set up to try to convert them to Christianity. Yet they changed the face of Britain.

This is a modern picture, but it is based on descriptions from the time.
Describe the navvies, mentioning their tools and their dress.
Look at the scene, then describe in detail how a railway line was built.

A Railway Journey

1 Waiting on the platform.

2 Loading the luggage.

3 Ready to go.

?? QUESTION ??

Look at pictures 1-9 (on pages 69-71).
 Make a list of all the different sights, sounds and smells that you might experience during a railway journey in the nineteenth century.

69

Chapter 4

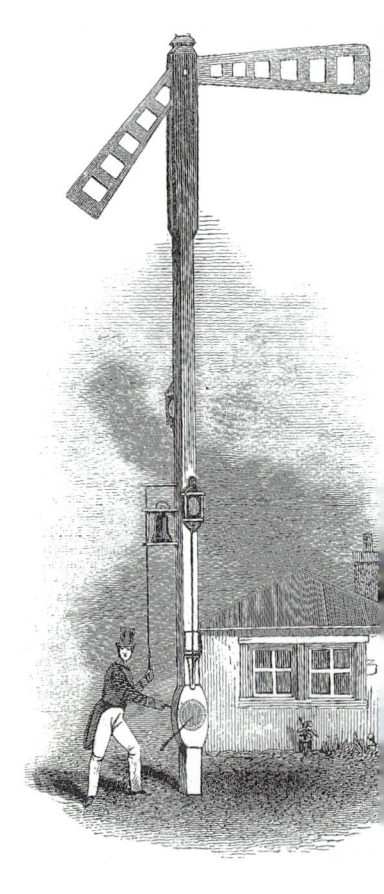

5 Signals.

6 Inside a railway carriage in 1855.

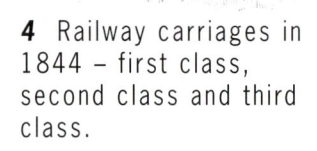

4 Railway carriages in 1844 – first class, second class and third class.

70

Changes in the Economy

7 Travelling by steam. Note the telegraph wires.

8 Journey's end.

9 Leaving the station.

Changing Attitudes

History books often give the impression that the nineteenth century was an era of cruelty, neglect and terrible suffering. But this is just not true. Many Victorians were caring people. We know about the bad conditions in the towns and factories because caring Victorians investigated them, SO THAT PARLIAMENT COULD CHANGE THINGS.

The Victorians invented the idea of the welfare state, whereby the government has a duty to take care of the people. After 1820, Parliament began to pass laws to make people's lives better.

Better Working Conditions

The **Factories Act** of 1833 improved conditions for children working in the mills.

The **Mines Act** of 1842 made it illegal to employ women and children in the mines. Most importantly of all, the Victorians introduced inspectors. There had been Factory Acts before 1833, but manufacturers had just ignored them; now government inspectors visited the factories to make sure they did not.

Conditions in the Towns

In 1835, the **Municipal Corporations Act** set up a system of town councils. **Public Health Acts** (in 1848 and 1875) forced councils to build sewers, provide clean water and clear away slums. But the councils did much more than what the law forced them to do. They competed with each other to pave and clean the streets. They built town halls, libraries and museums. They provided parks, dispensaries (for medicines), swimming baths, street lighting and a fire brigade.

Power to the People

The Victorians discovered the power of public opinion; in this sense, they might be said to have invented real democracy. At the same time, alongside the campaigns to improve working and living conditions, they campaigned to give more men the vote. In 1832, the **First Parliamentary Reform Act** abolished the rotten boroughs (see page 6) and gave the vote to a few more people.

Further reforms followed. In the 1840s, the Chartists campaigned for a number of changes which would allow working men to have a greater say in Parliament. Although they were unsuccessful, many of their demands eventually became law. The Parliamentary Reform Acts of 1867 and 1884 extended the vote to ALL men except lords, criminals and lunatics. Even more important was the 1872 **Ballot Act,** which allowed people to vote in secret.

After 1872, for the first time, British men could elect MPs who would represent them and try to carry out their wishes. In 1893, Keir Hardie, a Scotsman who had been a miner, formed the Independent Labour Party. Women, however, were still not allowed to vote.

Trade Unions

In 1824, the repeal of the **Combination Acts** allowed trade unions to exist legally. However, it was still illegal to take an oath when you joined the union. In 1834 six farm workers from the village of Tolpuddle in Dorset were transported to Australia for seven years when they swore on the Bible never to reveal the union's secrets. The case of the Tolpuddle Martyrs caused an outcry.

In 1837 they were given a free pardon and were allowed to come back home.

The first successful trade unions – called the New Model Unions – were set up in the 1850s. In 1875, the **Conspiracy Act** allowed union members to picket peacefully during a strike, and during the 1880s the lowest paid workers (for instance, the dockers) began to form strong unions.

Other Reforms
The **Prison Act** of 1824 improved conditions in the prisons. In 1829, Robert Peel created the Metropolitan (London) **Police Force**. Also, a number of acts were passed to make the law less harsh. In 1800 more than 200 offences carried the death penalty (for instance, stealing a handkerchief); by 1841, only murder and treason were punished by hanging. In 1857, transportation was abolished.

Slavery was abolished in the British Empire in 1833.

In 1834, the **New Poor Law** reorganised the system of poor relief. At first, it was a disaster; the poor hated the workhouses in which they were forced to live if they had no money. By the end of the century, however, the Poor Law had improved.

The **Education Act** of 1870 provided state-run Board Schools for all children. In 1876, education was made compulsory for all children under the age of 12. After 1891 it was provided free of charge.

The Victorians even cared for animals. The **RSPCA** was formed in 1824. Public animal fights were banned in 1835, and a number of acts were passed to prevent cruelty to animals. Fifty years later, in 1889, Parliament passed an **Act for the Prevention of Cruelty to Children**.

In the early years of the twentieth century there were further reforms, which mark the beginning of the Welfare State in Britain – the government introduced **pensions** in 1909, and **unemployment benefit** in 1911.

Board Schools in about 1900.

Women

Victorian men created an image of the 'perfect woman'. She was beautiful, demure, loving and intelligent. Such a woman would be worshipped by her husband, but she had few civil or political rights. Until 1884 a wife was officially listed as one of her husband's possessions. She had to do as she was told by her husband, who was her protector and adviser.

> **1 A woman's work**
>
> A woman should make a man's home delightful, and support him at his work. She should calm his mind – turn away his anger, and take away his sadness. Where a home is not happy, it is the woman's fault; for the woman, not the man, must make the sacrifice, especially in things that do not really matter . . . .
>
> In everything that women do, they must make it clear that they depend on men. There is something unpleasant about self-sufficiency in females . . . .
>
> Their sex should ever teach them to be subordinate; they must get their own way, not by arguing, but by a gentle appeal to love or right and wrong. In this respect, women are like children: the more they show they need looking after, the more attractive they are.
>
> **Mrs John Sandford**, *Woman in her Social and Domestic Character* (1837)

During the nineteenth century, women slowly gained civil rights. They wanted more control over their own lives. In 1900, however, they still did not have the vote.

Above: Woman's Mission – Companion of Manhood was painted in 1863.

In 1903 Emmeline Pankhurst founded the Women's Social and Political Union (WSPU). Her 'suffragettes' tried to win votes for women by force. They did not succeed; women were only given the vote in 1918, after the First World War.

QUESTIONS

1. Study source 1. List everything a woman was expected to do.
2. Study the picture, *Woman's Mission*. List all the ways in which it illustrates the view of women given in source 1.

It is hard to write about 'Victorian women' in general because all people are different. Sources 2 and 3 give contrasting views of the lives of women in the nineteenth century.

2 Real happiness

Sarah and Eliza were in good-natured delight over the clothes, from the lace wedding dress to the very last dozen embroidered pocket handkerchiefs . . . .

'Thirty dresses,' whispered Sarah as they went downstairs. 'The idea of a new dress every day for a month; now I call that real happiness.'

'Not such real, lasting happiness', answered Eliza, 'as eighteen bracelets, heaps of gloves and handkerchiefs . . . and to be going to be married'; and this wise conclusion brought them to the living-room door.

Emily Eden, *Semi-Attached Couple (1830)*

3 Discontent

While reading in the paper to Day on the subject on shorter houers of Labour I was Reminded of A cercomstance that came under my hone notis . . . .

I was Minding a masheen with 30 threds in it I was then maid to mind 2 of 30 treds each and with improved mecheens in A few years I was minding tow mecheens with tow 100 treds each and Dubel speed so that in our improved condation we went as if the Devel was After us for 10 houers per day and the feemals have often Been carred out fainting what with the heat and hard work and all this is Done in Christian England and then we are tould to Be content in the station of Life to wich the Lord as places us But I say the Lord never Did place us there so we have no Right to Be content . . . .

Letter from an unnamed woman (1873)

Chapter 5

Suffragettes

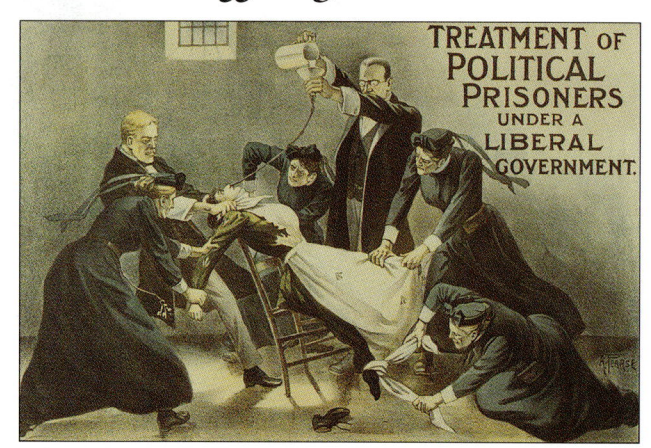

1 When put in prison, many suffragettes went on hunger strike. When they did this they were brutally force-fed.

2 A WSPU shop. It sold WSPU literature and goods such as Votes for Women chocolate, wrapped in the WSPU colours of purple, white and green.

3 Campaigning on a horse bus in 1910.

4 On Friday, 18 November 1910, suffragettes tried to force their way into the House of Commons. One hundred and twenty were arrested. Here, police take a stick from a militant suffragette.

5 Breaking shop windows in 1912.

6 Hatcham Church, in London, is burned down by militant suffragettes in 1913.

8 Suffragettes chained to railings in Downing Street, in 1913.

9 In the summer of 1913, thousands of suffragettes went on a six-week pilgrimage. They marched to London from all over the country. What do you notice about the sex of the people in the crowd?

10 In 1913, suffragettes demonstrated in Wales. They were attacked by Welsh men and had to be rescued by the police.

7 One suffragette, Emily Davison, threw herself under the king's horse on Derby Day, 4 June 1913.

Children's Comics

The Victorians invented childhood! In the eighteenth century, children had been dressed like small versions of their parents and were expected to behave like adults. It was the Victorians who realised that children are different, and that they need their own activities and toys. They encouraged children to play games such as cricket and hockey, to teach them the values of teamwork and fair play. It was also realised that children needed their own literature.

Early in the nineteenth century, many young people read adventure stories published in cheap magazines known as 'penny dreadfuls'. One example was *Sweeney Todd, the Demon Barber*. The longest, *Black Bess*, written by Edward Viles, was published over 254 weeks, and contained two and a half million words.

The stories in the penny dreadfuls were racy and violent. Adults complained that they were unsuitable for children and that they were badly printed, 'in a blurred, sight-destroying way'. Even fairy stories such as *Cinderella* came in for criticism: she was far too rebellious, and should have been content with her place in life as a servant! Towards the end of the nineteenth century, however, children's comics appeared which provided more acceptable stories for young people. The most famous, started in 1879, was *The Boy's Own Paper*. These comics became very popular, and they moulded the opinions of a generation of children.

What Were Children's Stories About?

The new comics contained stories which appealed to children, such as *Dick Turpin and the Pirate Queen*, *A Dead Man's Secret* (a detective story), *In Trackless Space*, and *Yo! Ho! For the Spanish Main*. Girls' comics carried stories such as *Galloping Gloria the Lady Turpin* and *Grace Daring the Girl Chauffeur*.

Although the new comics had exciting stories, the heroes never swore. They were honest, fair, brave – and above all, tough. One writer gave this passage as an example of the kind of story he had read in *The Boy's Own Paper*:

> It was the work of a moment to amputate MacNab's leg. A substitute was briskly carved from the nearest njama-tree by Sandy. MacNab at once leapt up and expressed himself ready to march all day. As he spoke, a shower of poisoned spears rattled through the bush.
> MacTavish gnawed his lip.
> **D.B. Wyndham-Lewis**, *The Tatler*

Attendance at school was compulsory after 1876, and it was a sign of the changing times that many children's stories were set in schools. These schools were filled with bullies to be defeated, and stupid teachers with silly names, who fell easy prey to any trick. Girls' schools, similarly, were full of 'jolly hockey sticks, swots, sneaks and topping gym mistresses'.

Towards the end of the nineteenth century, patriotic comics such as *Union Jack* appeared, with stories like *Fighting for the Flag*, about how the British defeated the Zulu tribes of South Africa.

As Europe slid towards the First World War in the years before 1914, comics began to include stories about Britain being invaded by a foreign power – usually

Russia or Germany. In 1908 the *Boys' Herald* explained why these countries wanted to destroy Britain:

> The Britisher is hated abroad. Why? Because of our huge possessions and colonies, because of our wealth as a nation, because of our enterprise and grit. Foreign nations are jealous of our progress.

Comics treated foreigners in a way we find offensive today. Foreigners were cheats and cowards who fought unfairly. They were often figures of fun, even if – like Ching-Ching the Chinese detective – they were clever in a devilish kind of way. Black people were referred to as 'niggers', and in the stories they usually spoke in a ridiculous pidgin English.

Women fared little better in boys' comics. They had to be robust, because they were always getting into the most dreadful scrapes, from which they had to be rescued by the daring hero. Women with sex appeal were to be avoided at all costs. In one story, the detective Sexton Blake faced the temptress Roxane, who asked him:

> 'Am I ugly? Am I repulsive? Am I lacking in intelligence? Other men have not found me so.'
> 'You are very lovely and very, very desirable,' said Blake in strained tones.
> 'Then why won't you . . .'
> He shook his head.
> 'No. I am sorry but I can't. My career would suffer.'
>
> *Union Jack*

The women in boys' comics might be pretty, but they always wore ankle-length skirts.

QUESTIONS

1. What did the author of the story in the *Union Jack* want to teach his young male readers about girls?
2. Writers used stories in comics to influence children's attitudes. Make a list of things that a child living before 1914 would have grown up believing.

INDEX

Acts of Parliament
    Ballot Act (1872) 72
    Combination Acts (1799) 8, 72
    Conspiracy Act (1875) 73
    Education Act (1870) 73
    Factories Act (1833) 72
    Habeas Corpus 8
    Mines Act (1842) 65, 72
    Municipal Corporations Act (1835) 72
    Navigation Acts (1651) 14
    New Poor Law (1834) 73
    Parliamentary Reform Act (1832) 72
    Parliamentary Reform Act (1867) 72
    Parliamentary Reform Act (1884) 72
    Prevention of Cruelty to Children Act (1889) 73
    Prison Act (1824) 73
    Public Health Acts (1848 and 1875) 35, 72
    Six Acts (1819) 9
Africa 15, 20, 21, 22-23, 24, 26, 27, 32, 33
Agricultural Revolution *see* Farming and food
American War of Independence 16-19
Australia 8, 14, 72

Black Hole of Calcutta 12-13
Boston Tea Party 16
British army and navy 14, 17, 18, 19
British Empire 11, 14-15, 16, 19, 32-33, 73, 79

Canals 66
Chartists 72
Children 2, 4, 5, 6-7, 20, 21, 22, 24, 25, 27, 30, 31, 35, 38, 40, 50, 53, 54, 55, 56, 58, 59, 61, 64, 65, 73, 78-79
Coal mining 58-65
Comics 78-79
Cotton 35, 53, 54, 57

Declaration of Independence 16
Disease and medicine 21, 28, 29, 32, 35, 38, 40-41, 51, 54, 60

Elections and voting 6, 8, 11, 72, 74, 76-77
Enclosure 46-47, 49

Farming and food 2, 11, 22, 34, 35, 42, 43-49, 67
France 13, 14-15, 16, 17
French Revolution 8

India 12-13, 14, 15, 32, 33
Industrial Revolution 11, 42, 52-71
Irish famine 50-51

Living conditions 2, 3-5, 11, 35, 38, 40-41, 67, 72

Middle Passage 21, 27-29

North America 14, 15, 30, 51

Parliament 6, 8, 14, 20, 47, 49, 51, 55, 56, 64, 72, 76
Pensions 73
Pentrich rebellion 8
People
    Arkwright, Richard 52
    Bakewell, Robert 46, 48
    Cartwright, Edmund 53
    Clive, Robert 12-13, 15
    Cook, Captain James 14
    Crompton, Samuel 53
    Darby, Abraham 60
    Davison, Emily 77
    Davy, Humphrey 60
    George III 6, 19
    Hargreaves, James 52
    Hogarth, William 3-5, 6-7
    Hunt, Henry 9
    Kay, John 52
    Malthus, Thomas 35
    Newcomen, Thomas 53
    Oliver, William 8
    Pankhurst, Emmeline 74
    Stephenson, George 67
    Townshend, 'Turnip' 46, 48, 49
    Trevithick, Richard 67
    Tull, Jethro 46, 48
    Washington, George 16, 17
    Watt, James 53, 67
    Wilberforce, William 20
    Wolfe, James 15
Peterloo 8-9
Police 73
Population 11, 34-35, 38

Railways 11, 32, 66-71
Reforms 11, 72-73
Religion 4, 23, 33, 68
RSPCA 73

Seven Years' War 15
Slave trade and slavery 11, 20-31, 73
Steam power 11, 53
Suffragettes 74, 76-77

Textile revolution 52-55, 56-57
Tolpuddle Martyrs 72-73
Trade 14, 15, 20-21, 23, 25, 30-31
Trade unions 8, 11, 72, 73
Transportation 8, 14, 72
Turnpike Trusts 66

Unemployment benefit 73

West Indies 20, 21, 26, 27, 30-31
Women and girls 6, 11, 20, 21, 22, 24, 25, 27, 30, 31, 38, 40, 50, 52, 53, 54, 55, 58, 64, 65, 68, 72, 74-77, 78, 79
Working conditions 8, 11, 35, 53, 54-57, 64-65, 68, 72